PRAISE FOR THE PLAY

REASONS TO BE HAPPY

"Mr. LaBute is more relaxed as a playwright than he's ever been. He is clearly having a good time revisiting old friends . . . you're likely to feel the same way . . . the most winning romantic comedy of the summer, replete with love talk, LaBute-style, which isn't so far from hate talk . . . "
—**Ben Brantley,** *The New York Times*

"These working-class characters are in fine, foul-mouthed voice, thanks to the scribe's astonishing command of the sharp side of the mother tongue. But this time the women stand up for themselves and give as good as they get."
—**Marilyn Stasio,** *Variety*

"LaBute has a keen ear for conversational dialogue in all its profane, funny and inelegant glory."
—**Joe Dziemianowicz,** *New York Daily News*

"LaBute . . . nails the bad faith, the grasping at straws, the defensive barbs that mark a tasty brawl."
—**Elisabeth Vincentelli,** *New York Post*

". . . intense, funny, and touching . . . In following up with the lives of his earlier characters, LaBute presents another compassionate examination of the ways people struggle to connect and try to find happiness."
—**Jennifer Farrar,** The Associated Press

". . . terrifically entertaining."
—**Philip Boroff,** *Bloomberg*

"[A] triumph . . . always electric with life. LaBute has a terrific way of demonstrating that even in their direst spoken punches . . . fighting lovers are hilarious. . . . completely convincing."
—**David Finkle,** *Huffington Post*

REASONS TO BE PRETTY

"Mr. LaBute is writing some of the freshest and most illuminating American dialogue to be heard anywhere these days . . . *Reasons* flows with the compelling naturalness of overheard conversation. . . . It's never easy to say what you mean, or to know what you mean to begin with. With a delicacy that belies its crude vocabulary, *Reasons to be Pretty* celebrates the everyday heroism in the struggle to find out."
—**Ben Brantley,** *The New York Times*

"[T]here is no doubt that LaBute knows how to hold an audience. . . . LaBute proves just as interesting writing about human decency as when he is writing about the darker urgings of the human heart." —**Charles Spencer**, *Telegraph*

"[F]unny, daring, thought-provoking . . ." —**Sarah Hemming**, *Financial Times*

IN A DARK DARK HOUSE

"Refreshingly reminds us . . . that [LaBute's] talents go beyond glibly vicious storytelling and extend into thoughtful analyses of a world rotten with original sin." —**Ben Brantley**, *The New York Times*

"LaBute takes us to shadowy places we don't like to talk about, sometimes even to think about . . ." —**Erin McClam**, *Newsday*

WRECKS

"Superb and subversive . . . A masterly attempt to shed light on the ways in which we manufacture our own darkness. It offers us the kind of illumination that Tom Stoppard has called 'what's left of God's purpose when you take away God.'" —**John Lahr**, *The New Yorker*

"[*Wrecks* is a] tasty morsel of a play . . . The profound empathy that has always informed LaBute's work, even at its most stringent, is expressed more directly and urgently than ever here." —**Elysa Gardner**, *USA Today*

"*Wrecks* is bound to be identified by its shock value. But it must also be cherished for the moment-by-moment pleasure of its masterly portraiture. There is not an extraneous syllable in LaBute's enormously moving love story." —**Linda Winer**, *Newsday*

FAT PIG

"The most emotionally engaging and unsettling of Mr. LaBute's plays since *bash* . . . A serious step forward for a playwright who has always been most comfortable with judgmental distance." —**Ben Brantley**, *The New York Times*

"One of Neil LaBute's subtler efforts . . . Demonstrates a warmth and compassion for its characters missing in many of LaBute's previous works [and] balances black humor and social commentary in a . . . beautifully written, hilarious . . . dissection of how societal pressures affect relationships [that] is astute and up-to-the-minute relevant." —**Frank Scheck**, *New York Post*

THE DISTANCE FROM HERE

"LaBute gets inside the emptiness of American culture, the masquerade, and the evil of neglect. *The Distance from Here*, it seems to me, is a new title to be added to the short list of important contemporary plays."

—**John Lahr**, *The New Yorker*

THE MERCY SEAT

"Though set in the cold, gray light of morning in a downtown loft with inescapable views of the vacuum left by the twin towers, *The Mercy Seat* really occurs in one of those feverish nights of the soul in which men and women lock in vicious sexual combat, as in Strindberg's *Dance of Death* and Edward Albee's *Who's Afraid of Virginia Woolf.*"   —**Ben Brantley**, *The New York Times*

"[A] powerful drama . . . LaBute shows a true master's hand in gliding us amid the shoals and reefs of a mined relationship." —**Donald Lyons**, *New York Post*

THE SHAPE OF THINGS

"LaBute . . . continues to probe the fascinating dark side of individualism . . . [His] great gift is to live in and to chronicle that murky area of not-knowing, which mankind spends much of its waking life denying."

—**John Lahr**, *The New Yorker*

"LaBute is the first dramatist since David Mamet and Sam Shepard—since Edward Albee, actually—to mix sympathy and savagery, pathos and power."

—**Donald Lyons**, *New York Post*

"*Shape* . . . is LaBute's thesis on extreme feminine wiles, as well as a disquisition on how far an artist . . . can go in the name of art . . . Like a chiropractor of the soul, LaBute is looking for realignment, listening for a crack." —**John Istel**, *Elle*

BASH

"The three stories in *bash* are correspondingly all, in different ways, about the power instinct, about the animalistic urge for control. In rendering these narratives, Mr. LaBute shows not only a merciless ear for contemporary speech but also a poet's sense of recurring, slyly graduated imagery . . . darkly engrossing."

—**Ben Brantley**, *The New York Times*

NEIL LABUTE is an award-winning playwright, filmmaker, and screen-writer. His plays include: *bash*, *The Shape of Things*, *The Distance From Here*, *The Mercy Seat*, *Fat Pig* (Olivier Award nominated for Best Comedy), *Some Girl(s)*, *Reasons to be Pretty* (Tony Award nominated for Best Play), *In A Forest, Dark and Deep*, a new adaptation of *Miss Julie,* and *Reasons to be Happy*. He is also the author of *Seconds of Pleasure*, a collection of short fiction, and a 2013 recipient of a Literature Award from the American Academy of Arts and Letters.

Neil LaBute's films include *In the Company of Men* (New York Critics' Circle Award for Best First Feature and the Filmmaker Trophy at the Sundance Film Festival), *Your Friends and Neighbors*, *Nurse Betty*, *Possession*, *The Shape of Things*, *Lakeview Terrace*, *Death at a Funeral, Some Velvet Morning,* and *Dirty Weekend*.

Things We Said Today

short plays and monologues by neil labute

overlook duckworth
new york • london

This edition first published in the United States and the United Kingdom
in 2014 by Overlook Duckworth, Peter Mayer Publishers, Inc.

New York
141 Wooster Street
New York, NY 10012
www.overlookpress.com
For bulk and special sales, please contact sales@overlookny.com,
or write us at above address.

London
30 Calvin Street
London E1 6NW
info@duckworth-publishers.co.uk
www.ducknet.co.uk
For bulk and special sales, please contact sales@duckworth-publishers.co.uk,
or write us at the above address.

Cataloging-in-Publication Data is available from the Library of Congress

Book design and type formatting by Bernard Schleifer
Manufactured in the United States of America
US ISBN 978-1-4683-0977-5
UK ISBN 978-0-7156-4934-3
1 3 5 7 9 10 8 6 4 2

for jo bonney & eric bogosian

where are you going, where have you been?
joyce carol oates

Contents

Preface

"What're you writing these days?"

That's the question I get asked more often than not by people
I know—some well and others hardly at all. People, in particular
journalists, always want to know the next thing you're working on,
often before the film or play or TV show that you're talking to them
about has even been released or performed or televised. People like
to be "in the know," I suppose—or they're just really fucking nosy
(which is actually more what I believe to be the case).

The following collection is a pretty fair representation of what
I've been writing these days, for the stage, the screen (both large and
small) and the Internet. I'm a big believer in work—and I mean actual
"work," like the rolling up your sleeves and getting your hands dirty
kind of work—and as much as I despise the self-promoting
aspects of Twitter and Facebook and Instagram, I also love the fact
that more venues than ever have opened up as places for folks to
display their creative endeavors to the public (like YouTube, for
example). I have no shame about it, in fact—I am as glad to see my
work done well by an actor or a filmmaker on my laptop as I am to
watch it in a theatre or cinema in New York City or London or Paris.
Mind you, this can also be a danger, as sometimes the first interaction a person might have with my material is a scene or monologue

online that is done by someone too young or too old or just not right for the part and that is that, that's what they will think forever of my work as a whole based on the one clip that they find on a website somewhere. Still, all in all, I think it's worth the risk.

In fact, two of the monologues included in this volume began life as part of a series of monologues created as an Internet collection called "My America" for the 50th anniversary celebration at Center Stage Theatre in Baltimore, Maryland. It was the brainchild of the talented writer/director turned artistic director Kwame Kwei-Armah, who allowed me to do two pieces for the anthology (which uses 50 different playwrights to tell 50 different American stories). The entire thing was filmed by the great American auteur Hal Hartley and we were lucky enough to land Bobby Cannavale and Gia Crovatin to breathe life into the two characters. While the pieces were also seen on screen or performed live at the theatre, all of the short films first sprang to life on the Center Stage website and it was thrilling to see this work done so well by so many wonderful writers and actors; it became a nice place for me to sneak away to and escape into a wonderful world of new characters and new stories.

That, however, was not my first foray into seeing my work done professionally on the World Wide Web (does anyone but me still call it that?) The short play *Call Back*—which has been done on stage in Los Angeles and New York City—began as a short film entitled *Denise* for a web channel called WIGS (on YouTube) that was given artistic birth by the talented multi-hyphenates Rodrigo Garcia and Jon Avnet. The idea behind it was to generate new series and short films that had a single governing principle: to create more and better roles for women. The list of top actresses who have taken part in the endeavor is astounding and they're still going strong. I wrote *Denise* for them (starring the amazing Alison Pill and the equally wonderful

Chris Messina); it was directed by a terrific new director, Lee Toland Krieger. I love what they did with the script and it's fantastic to be able to send people a link that allows them to access this work at the click of a button. Vimeo and Dropbox have become my new local video store and I can live with this particular technological advancement quite easily, thank you very much.

The other short plays in this collection had very eclectic journeys to the stage. *Good Luck (In Farsi)* was another in a series of pieces that I've written for the short play festival "Summer Shorts" that takes place in New York each summer (and is overseen by two great theatre artists, J.J. Kandel and John McCormack). I wanted to write something for them that I don't do very often: a comedy for an entirely female cast. It was also the first time that I was able to direct a show for this very enjoyable venture and I would love to do it again—there are few greater pleasures than having a play running in New York City during the summer months. (I can already think of a few things that I like more, but believe me it's a really nice feeling.)

Squeeze Play is probably one of the most unusual pieces in this book—not due to the work itself but because of the company that commissioned it. This is the second piece I've written for the Mile Square Theatre in Hoboken, New Jersey. They do an annual benefit called "7th Inning Stretch" and every play in the event is baseball-themed. Well, I like a challenge as much as the next person so I've been a part of this extravaganza twice now (the first was a piece called *I Love This Game,* which I adapted into one of the monologues now in this collection under the *Ten x Ten* banner). One of my favorite New York actors and a veteran of many of my short plays, Victor Slezak, graciously played the part of the "Coach."

Pick One had its debut at the Edinburgh Theatre Festival (followed by a run at the Young Vic theatre in London)—it was another piece I wrote for the ambitious and politically-minded young company called "Theatre Uncut," which is based in the UK and helmed by Emma Callander and Hannah Price. They commission plays that are performed in Britain first and then made available to actors everywhere to perform for free, usually during the month of November. The guiding principle of this particular set of plays was the question: "Do we all get more 'right wing' in hard times?" My response to their query is included within these pages. It's a simple, nasty little piece of work but it made perfect sense to me at the time—after all, the Nazis sat around and ate lunch while they were dreaming up their "Final Solution."

Last and certainly not least is the new one-act *The Possible*. I'm most embarrassed about this little playlet because of where its life began—it is the first thing I wrote for a short play festival that has been named after me and takes place each summer in St. Louis, Missouri. Don't get me wrong; it's a very nice thing and the man who started the festival, William Roth, is a lovely and dedicated actor/impresario doing strong work in the great Midwest (a place I know and love). I'm just someone who tends to hide behind his notebook and would rather be off writing or sitting in a dark theatre than having a play festival named after him but hey, it happened, it's out there and it's one more place for people to see theatre so who am I to complain? When I attended the event last year I saw some good theatre, met some wonderful people and really appreciated the hard work that went into something that I hope will continue for many years to come. *The Possible* is a fun play, too, when done well and it certainly was in Missouri by an excellent director and pair of local actors.

The other ten monologues in *Things We Said Today* are pieces I wrote for a unique series of short films that I was very fortunate to do for DirecTV. I created a television series for them previously as well—a series of mini-dramas called *Full Circle* that all took place in the same restaurant—but I wasn't able to be involved with that venture during its production period, so the second time around I both wrote and directed all ten films. I cast an exceptional group of actors and was able to film each monologue in an uninterrupted take and in glorious black and white with the help of the great Dutch cinematographer Rogier Stoffers. Louisa Krause, Adam Brody, Maggie Grace, Fred Weller, Jenna Fischer, Jason Patric, Amy Madigan, Richard Kind, Judith Light and Bill Pullman lifted the words off the respective pages and did that thing that talented actors do: make you look good and the material look better. I was blessed to have them all and also the backing and belief of two good executive producers, Tim Harms and Andrew Carlberg. The real heroes of *Ten x Ten*, however, are Bart Peters and Chris Long at DirecTV, who have set out to do what I consider to be the most original content I've currently seen or been a part of on cable television.

I'm a lucky man and happy to be involved in their particular cultural renaissance.

The *Ten x Ten* monologues are meant to be a collection of stories across a group of different men and women who speak openly about love and lust. I'm very happy with what we've been able to achieve with the short films and I hope the pieces turn out to be useful tools in the hands of other students and actors (or simply just fun to read).

I suppose, in the end, that's what this collection consists of: work that I think will be of worth to people in my beloved industry who are out there constantly searching for new material to perform, new challenges to take on, new roles to create.

Know that I admire what you do and respect it, too. It's easy to sit back and criticize; anybody with a fake email address or an arts blog can tell you how good or bad you are. They, however, are not the brave ones who get up in front of an audience with their efforts and say "*Here*. Take a look at *this*. This is *me*. This is what *I* can do."

These cowards take free tickets and pass out "two thumbs down" or "three stars" to the artists living and working on the front lines of the creative divide. Do yourself a favor and don't listen to their snarky asides and comments. Listen to yourself. Listen to people you trust and, most important, keep doing what you're doing and I promise you that I will keep on doing the same.

We may not change the world but, hey, I'll bet we at least leave behind a mark.

—Neil LaBute
March 2014

Ten x Ten

Ten x Ten monologues were shot in New York City (December 2013) and Los Angeles (January 2014) and were originally aired on the *Audience* channel on DirecTV. They were all written and directed by Neil LaBute. The cast was as follows: Adam Brody *(Man - 20s)*; Louisa Krause *(Woman - 20s)*; Fred Weller *(Man - 30s)*; Maggie Grace *(Woman - 30s)*; Jason Patric *(Man - 40s)*; Jenna Fischer *(Woman - 40s)*; Richard Kind *(Man - 50s)*; Amy Madigan *(Woman - 50s)*; Bill Pullman *(Man - 60s)*; Judith Light *(Woman - 60s)*.

The monologues for *Woman - 20s* and *Man - 40s* were previously published in alternative versions under the respective titles *Bad Girl* and *I Love This Game*.

man - 20s

A MAN *in his twenties. Looking at us.*

MAN . . . I hate my hair! Look at it. It's on its way out; I mean, you can tell that, right? I'm losing my hair . . . in my *20s*. Another couple years, it'll be gone . . . that totally sucks. Doesn't it? Yeah. Shit. That's— (*Beat.*) And my mom told me that it would, she warned me about this, way back when I was a kid . . . she would look at my hairline after I got it trimmed, over at one of those cheap places that she used to take me to—SuperCuts or something crappy like that—and she'd study my scalp and the patterns fanning out from the top of my head—the "crown," I think it's called—she could look at those few things on a person and tell you stuff about yourself . . . or your future, at least. And so she said that to me . . . several times . . . that I was gonna go bald. Well, I mean . . . she never said that. Moms don't say things like that, not to their kids . . . some moms probably do, *bad* moms, moms who are mean or angry about something in their own lives and so they lash out at people, their own kids even, just because they're unhappy or sad or whatever. Moms like that might say that to their sons—"you're going bald"—but not mine. She'd call it "fine." Look at my hair and touch it with those lovely, thin hands of hers and say it was "fine." "You have very fine hair." When

I was a really small kid, not even in school yet and she'd say that, I thought she meant that it was "nice." Like how that word can be used to mean a good thing. "Fine jewelry" or that type of thing. I felt like I had this head full of beautiful fine hair, as if it was all spun gold or something . . . kids are so dumb, right? I guess *I* was, anyway, when it came to my mom . . . (*Beat.*) But later on I came to realize that all she meant was I was gonna lose it at some point in my life. My hair. (*Beat.*) I haven't yet . . . I mean, seems to be hanging in there for now . . . have to help it out a little bit with a few products and, you know . . . a crazy sort of *judicious* arranging—combing it all forward and then to the side and then back . . . silly shit that you make up as you're trying to have it all look like everything's cool, everything's fine—it's such a crock, anyway, right? *Hair*. Why we place such a high value on it in society and that kind of thing. But we do, though, right? There's no question that we do . . . our hair and our looks and, and, like . . . you know . . . money and youth, everything. All that. It's just so dumb. (*Beat.*) Unless you have 'em all! And then it's amazing! I'm kidding, but . . . sort of. No, if you have those things, or even a few of them . . . a lot of cash or some great-looking face, a body that everybody wants or that type of thing . . . then it's all ok and you just go with it. Enjoy it while you can, I suppose. It's natural. It's a gift and so you take it and run with it and the rest of us are left in your wake to grumble and moan. That's life. But for a guy like me—someone who grew up with a very normal set of parents and without a fancy house or upbringing and not amazing-looking or a sportsman, none of the kinds of advantages I was talking about earlier—or *bemoaning*, really—to have this very average face and body and job and all of that . . . to then have your hair start to go at this young age . . . that just, you know, it kinda stinks. It's not fair.

It makes me mad. (*Beat.*) And it's not like I'm an old man, a grand-
father or whatever, and then you expect it to happen . . . this is me
dealing with it when I should be out on the beach and driving a
sports car and all that shit . . . it's a cliche but that's the sort of
thing I should be doing . . . and instead I'm always looking in
store windows and messing with my part while I try to camouflage
my . . . you know what I'm saying. That's what I'm doing as a
young man. Fixing my hair. Watching those damn Rogaine commercials and seriously thinking about finding a hat that I can wear
on all occasions . . . one of those stupid hats like you see the hip-
ster guys wear around—most of them being bald as well and just
pretending that they love hats, that they absolutely would choose
to wear this thing even if they weren't hiding a huge fucking bald
patch on the top of their head. "No, I'm not kidding, I seriously
love *fedoras.*" I mean, come on! Please. Nobody does . . . not
Bruce Willis, not you or me. Guys do it because they're going
bald and, worse, they think that girls won't like it. That they'll find
them less masculine if they are losing their hair . . . especially
when they're younger. Like me. (*Beat.*) I mean, obviously there
must be a few guys out there—a very small percentage of, just,
like, total assholes who think they look "cool" in a hat and so they
trot 'em out every so often, for a party or whatnot—but that's a
super small part of the real population, I think. It *has* to be—and
if I see a guy in a hat, one of those with a brim on it that's kind of
flipped up, and a *feather* in the band or some kind of *fun* material
around it—I'm about 85% certain that the guy's a total dick. A real
jerk. And I am so rarely not right about that fact that it's not even
worth noting the times I was wrong. So I can't do that . . . can't
wear a hat with any serious authority . . . even though I've been
feeling so desperate lately that I've had a moment or two where

I've considered it. Tried a few on. It's gotten *that* bad . . . (*Beat.*)
No, seriously, I'm gonna have to do something one day soon,
I really will. I'll cut it short or grow it out—not like a loser ponytail
guy, not like that, but a bit longer so I have some volume to play
with . . . something. I dunno. I'll *have* to. (*Beat.*) I think my last
girlfriend left me because of it—she'd say no if you asked her,
stopped her in the street and made her tell you why, but deep
down I think it was that. My hair. She'd probably say it was my
general . . . I'm not sure . . . some attitude thing I've got or that
I have jumped around from job to job lately, which is true but not
terrible and lots of people do that—it's called "finding yourself,"
thank you very much—and just a load of other crap that Katja
would be willing to tell you if you asked her . . . she's from Latvia,
not that it matters but that's why she has the exotic name and this
kind of *thing* about her when you talk to her . . . this edge. This
privileged sort of edge that isn't based in reality since she comes
from a farm in a country that Russia doesn't even want any more
. . . but that was Katja. She'd be happy to do that if you asked,
list off my faults for you . . . but honestly I think she was turned
off by my hair. Yep. (*Beat.*) So many guys today are going with the
buzzed look, the totally close-cut thing or a completely shaved
head and that's fine, I can do it, but I think it's a cop-out. Person-
ally. I do. You know you're doing it because the hair is going—
I don't care if you're the guy in the movies . . . what's his name . . .
the one with the . . . Jason Statham? Is that it? Him or my next-
door neighbor who does it every other day. Shaves it off. That's a
way of getting around the fact that your hair sucks and it's gone
and you think it looks shitty and so you do that. That's what that
is. (*Beat.*) Only person who is fine with it . . . and I mean totally
A-OKAY with it . . . is my mom. She doesn't care at all. Looks at

me with nothing but love, however I look. I mean, she knows that it bugs me so she's worried and she'll cut out little articles or tell me about a paid program she saw on television, two in the morning . . . but she doesn't care. At all. That woman loves me . . . and that feels so damn good. So great. (*Beat.*) I mean, fuck, if I could find somebody who loved me like that, some girl who looked at me like she does—fat, thin, ugly or from darkest Africa—I wouldn't care at all. I'd be hers forever. Does it sound weird for me to say that? I mean . . . it's okay to love your mom, right? And I am not saying sexually, no, Jesus, I mean the "idea" of her. Who she is and what she represents. The way she makes me as person feel . . . loved. That's what I need in my life. A woman like that. (*Beat.*) I think that's absolutely okay. It is. To say that and feel it. To want a lady who loves me like she does . . . looks at me like Mom does. I honestly don't feel funny at all saying that to you. That I want that and am looking for that in my life. I'm not ashamed of it. I'm not. I'm *not*. (*Beat.*) I'm seriously not . . .

He stops talking for a moment. Looks at us. Nods. Looks away.

THE END.

woman - 20s

A WOMAN *in her twenties. Looking at us.*

WOMAN . . . I broke up with a guy not all that long ago so I'm, you
know . . . yeah. I'm not really ready for too much of anything but
it's just kinda, I dunno . . . weird, even at my age, to be without
someone. To not at least have that man who calls me up and
wants to take me out, even if I can't make it . . . maybe that's all
I need. Is that. Someone to want me, or . . . (*Beat.*) What I *used* to
do, and this is so childish, I realize that—but if I had a relationship
end . . . and I mean if, like, *he* ran out on me or that type of thing,
cheated with someone: I would go out a few nights later to the
bars and look around—it didn't matter where—could even be at
a restaurant or maybe a car dealer or wherever, and I'd find—
there is no way I should be telling you this!—I'd go after the
biggest loser in the place and then I'd fuck him. Yeah. Not as a
revenge or, or, you know, anything like that—and I'm not saying
the ugliest one or a mean guy, an asshole or anyone of that
nature—but just the guy who you'd spot—and you can find this
kind of person in nearly any place you go, the laundromat or at,
maybe a coffee shop . . . places like that are good—and I'd go
right over to him and offer myself up. (*Beat.*) I don't mean like it
was obvious or anything, not like "Here I am, take me now" or shit

like that but just be really really nice to him and laugh at his jokes
maybe, let him ask me out to dinner or even to a film—you can't
imagine some of the shit I've seen with these guys, like with the
subtitles at the bottom and all that! Ohhhh Jesus, I thought I was
gonna die a few times—but that's what I'd do. I would do that.
Go out on the date and then back over to his place, if he had one,
and then let him fuck me. Fuck me as many times as he could or,
or wanted to . . . do anything he might ever dream up—trust me,
a man like the kind I'm saying here is not all that super-inventive,
they just feel so lucky to be even near you that they cum, like, in
two seconds most of the time and spend the rest of the evening
on the edge of the bed apologizing to you. Seriously. (*Beat.*) Never
twice, though, ok? Don't be . . . that mistake is one I've made so
don't do it. It's not even, I dunno, not that it's *so* bad or like you're
starting up some sort of relationship or anything, but if you see
that kind of guy again—any kind at all, really, but definitely the
needier ones—then you're just getting yourself in deeper. You
know? I mean, I saw this one again, type I mentioned, took me
to the local *aquarium* or some deal and then out for ice creams—
whatever—we fucked that night. Like I said, how I described.
Fine. Something in me, though, and I've tried to go back and track
it down, see what it was that was so different about him but, see,
I left him my number. Yep. And of course, I mean, yes, he calls
me again—picked another moment where I was feeling low about
something, might have been about work or, shit, I dunno, but
I said alright, yeah, that I'd see him for a second time. I think his
name was Chip. Yes, it was, because when I heard it I was, like,
"Fuck, what? *Chip*?" Anyways, we go to Six Flags (you know, with
all those rides and games and things) which is pretty fun, I have
to admit, and the whole time he's a complete gentleman . . . no

sense of a "date" where I have to hold his hand or be all smiley, no, we're just laughing and . . . eating pizza and a ton of good stuff, *but*: back at his apartment that night, he's totally different. I'm serious. Just more, and this is slightly, that's all, just slightly, but still—wants me to undress in front of him and a little rougher going inside me, just a few things that a girl would notice, he's like that this time. *And* he tricks me! He does, he totally turns a blow-job around on me where I've been really specific in that I don't swallow—I mean, only for a guy who's, not even just special but like "the one," you know? "Him." *Marriage*-guy. *Super* cute. *Super* rich. *Super* smart. That type of person . . . somebody who is, like, a game-changer and that is not Chip. Chip's not even in the *minor* leagues of the kind of guy I'm talking about here . . . he's the "Oh shit . . . it's two a.m. I should think about finding a guy for tonight" sort of person . . . that's who Chip is . . . not a big-league player like I'm looking for if I choose to gulp down his stuff. Does that make sense? It *must* . . . you must understand exactly what I'm saying because those are my rules and they're really not that much different than most girls I know, so I'm guessing you know exactly what I'm talking about. Of course you do, you have to. And *Chip* certainly does . . . he totally gets it, knows his place in the food chain . . . I mean, I've told him already, this Chip, he *definitely* knows the rules and he says "Okay, no problem" and so I trust him to follow the guidelines and whatever, to just do his thing and then, you know . . . right? But Chip gets all, I mean, he is totally shallow breathing me here, as if we've just started and he could go on for however long and then he's, like, blam! He quivers and shoots a quart of his . . . I don't even like *thinking* about it, so imagine when it goes everywhere: mouth, my face, Stones T-shirt I'm wearing . . . ppplllttt! O-kay, that's

lovely! *And* as I look up at him, getting ready to head off to the
bathroom to clean up, he has this look on his face. Not a smile,
it's not quite that, but in his eyes, this . . . sort of a *gleam* or something. The way a regular guy might look at me if he'd done that.
Some good-looking guy who gets away with that kinda shit in bed
or even life because of his face or what he does for a living or
maybe his family . . . Chip is sitting there, off in the shadows and
watching me, with this faint little grin and his pupils flaring up . . .
excited by what he's just done to me. We don't say a word about
it to each other and I leave not that much later *but* he hardly even
seems interested in me after that—with these big yawns and
this continuous stream of "I have to work in the morning" just to
let me know I wasn't invited to stay over. My Stones shirt is
ruined and I'm sure I definitely downed some of his nasty jizz
and *that's* what I get from my second date with Chip? I'm not
welcome to sleep over for a few hours? That's nice. So I'm just
saying, and your life is your own so do what you wanna, but hey:
beware. Okay? However, if you wanna fuck someone so so
grateful the first time around . . . and I'm saying, like, in tears
and shit . . . *that* type of grateful, then you so have to screw a guy
like the ones I was mentioning earlier. You really really do. But
yeah, be careful—just the one time. Oh, and they will totally eat
your pussy, and as many times as you ask them to, so that's
something—not that they know what they're doing down there
but most times it's still good enough to be at least ok. I mean,
end of the day, it's just *licking*, right? Anybody can do it. (*Beat.*)
But yeah. That's what I've done sometimes . . . when I'm feeling
down or I find out the dude I'm with is actually married, I'll go do
that. I mean, I don't end up *dating* 'em or anything, I'm not crazy!
Right? It's just a little thing that I'll do, like a habit, or, or, or—

I dunno, what else would you call it? A hobby, maybe. Yeah, like that. This thing you do every so often, makes ya feel good about yourself, nobody's the wiser. It's a *hobby*. (*Beat.*) I know it's not the best thing, it's probably pretty dangerous and crap like that, too, I know that, so I do try and curb that side of me these days, I really really do. But sometimes I can't help it . . . I'm a bad girl. And honestly, there is nothing like a super lame guy with his cock inside of you and *sobbing* as he goes to make you feel pretty alright about yourself. It's true. (*Beat.*) . . . hey, I'm not pretending it's the smart choice or, or, like, the most *adult* thing to do in the world. I'm just saying that it works for *me*. Ok? (*Beat.*) Alright then. Jesus . . .

She stops talking for a moment. Looks at us. Nods. Looks away.

THE END.

man - 30s

A MAN *in his thirties. Looking at us.*

MAN   . . . I was on a plane recently. I was going to someplace—
obviously . . . I mean, I know that's obvious, but—I was flying
there and I read most of the way, a book I had, and some magazines that they've got there in that *pocket* . . . but for about the
first hour of the flight—I don't even know if it was that long . . .
45 minutes, maybe—I turned my laptop on. I realized they had
wi-fi and I thought I'd catch up on a few emails, look at the news,
whatever . . . and at some point I hit one of those ads that pop up
on your computer without you doing anything to make it happen.
You know what I'm talking about, right . . . for insurance or *Viagra*
or, like . . . I dunno, a bunch of stuff . . . but they come on when
you happen to roll over them and that's it, nothing you can do,
they just come on and blast out their product at a really high level
of volume. You have to click 'em off to stop 'em . . . you know
what I'm saying, I know you've seen 'em before. Everybody has.
(*Beat.*) Anyway, this happens and I let it play for a second—I'm
serious, it's like a few moments when a guy is talking about this
and that, asking me to sell my gold for cash, I don't know, something stupid like that—and a voice next to me rings out, I get this
tap on the shoulder. Some woman looking up at me with this long,

straight hair and a really plain face—not unattractive but plain—
you know exactly the kind of girl I mean when I say that . . . she's
asking me to turn it down or if I have earphones or something.
The look on her face is like—and this is absolutely our first
moment of interaction onboard the plane, she's never once given
me the time of day since we sat down next to each other. Not
once. I'm not saying I was super-friendly with her, either—it's the
first flight out in the morning, like, 6 a.m. or something like that—
but still, I smiled at her when I got in my seat, a nod at least, but
this wall of silence from her. The whole time. She's working on
her computer from before we take off until we land—had kind of
a little thing with the flight attendant as we're getting set to go,
a bit of "I HAVE to send this email first . . ." or that sort of deal, bags
all over the floor in front of us, and she's clacking away on a Dell
computer doing pie charts and all these growth reports for some
fancy make-up or hair products company—none of which she
seems to use, mind you, she really is not beautiful, this woman—
but she's got the gall to say that to me: "Do you have any head-
phones?" Over something I didn't even do! I mean . . . people are
funny sometimes, aren't they? I think so . . . (*Beat.*) Right after she
knew I was unhappy with what she's said because I turn and look
her over, a couple blinks, before I say to her: "Is this bothering
you? It's just a *commercial* . . . it's not like I've got a movie on or
something . . . sorry." And not another word in return. Nothing.
Just a look from that face of hers. Staring up at me. (*Beat.*) Whatever. (*Beat.*) I don't even know what it was about her that I found
so annoying, but something . . . her face, I guess. That face of
hers. Just so . . . you know? Annoying . . . (*Beat.*) So I do the work
I'm doing, just few little things, being careful not to *bother* my
neighbor again—I even turn the volume down and, I mean,

I've never done that for anybody, NOBODY, ever—and at some point I nod off. I fall asleep. In my dream I have this elaborate fantasy in which this woman next to me, the plain one I was just telling you about . . . in my fantasy I see what my life would be like if we ended up together. It's a bit like one of those VISA commercials where you see everything passing before your eyes: dating and marriage and a few kids and all that, I'm seeing how things would go if me and this woman became husband and wife . . . but at the same time, because of what she's done to me and, you know, her looks . . . I'm also imaginging—or dreaming, I guess, the whole thing's really a dream and not some *lucid* thing that I should be feeling responsible for—but I imagine all the bad stuff I'd do to her as well. All the women I'd cheat on her with and the late nights out with my friends and how we'd end up divorced so many years later and all that. (*Beat.*) That's the dream I have about her, because of the way she treated me. (*Beat.*) There's a period there where apparently I sleep with some friends of hers from the sub-division we move into and . . . I dunno . . . a few times it seems like maybe I don't come home at night, not straight home, anyway . . . she drives me to drink is what it feels like now, when I think back on it . . . I am forced to become a bit of an alcoholic due to our lousy relationship and I also gamble a bit, I feel like that happened, too, now that I think about it. I kinda go to pot, if you wanna know the truth. I do . . . but, see, it's all because of her! This woman I never said one bad thing to and then she acts like that to me because of who she is and this sort of chip on her shoulder—I mean, that's what the whole problem seems to be, if you want to hear my opinion about it—she's got a chip on her shoulder toward the whole world due to her face, the one that God gave her. Not me. Not anybody else. God. Well, I suppose her parents, too, but a lot of it is God or Fate or whatever else you believe in. *That's* the problem but she's going around taking it out on people like you and me and so both of us—her and me, I'm saying, not you—we end up having a kind of pretty crappy life because of it. (*Beat.*) Now, I guess that really isn't a *fantasy*, per se, is it? Not technically. Fantasy would seem to have some sort of a more positive spin usually . . . at least that's how I think of it. Right? A "fantasy" is like imagining yourself with Marilyn Monroe or winning a baseball game, that kind of deal . . . and this is not that . . . it has nothing to do with that. Heroics or sleeping with some hot girl. This is my mind getting back at this woman who has a shitty attitude and made me feel bad for no good reason, that is what this is. (*Beat.*) Anyway, I wake up a little later, she's still chugging away on those pie charts and graphs and shit . . . does the same thing with the flight attendant as we're getting ready to land: "I'm putting it away right now, I am, I just HAVE to finish . . ." blah-blah-blah. Unbelievable, this one is. I mean, seriously. And the second the wheels touch the ground, she has two phones out—a Blackberry plus a different one, an iPhone, maybe—and she is clicking away and checking messages. Funny thing was—and this is what they call Karma or Kismet or one of those—she gets out of her belt and stands up before we're even parked at the gate . . . I mean, we're there, but not settled, you know what I mean? Not stopped. She gets up and opens her bin—one of the attendants is starting to say something to her but she's up and opens the thing and BAM! Her little Tumi bag, one of the over-the-shoulder kind, drops right out and on her foot. WHAM! Like a falling rock in a nature video from television. Right down onto her foot—and yes, she's got her shoes off, for comfort, no doubt—so the thing lands squarely on her toes. SMASH!

She sort of screams or whatever, kind of a yelp or something—
I wouldn't be surprised if it fractured a bone, hairline or other-
wise—but what's funny is, she looks straight at me when she
does it. Not down at her foot or up at the bin where it came from
or for help from the flight people . . . no. She looks right over into
my eyes. Like she *knew* this was payback for how she's treated
me. And I don't say a word. No, not one thing. I just smile at her.
The tiniest little grin and that's it. A faint little smirk that says,
"How do you like them apples?" (*Smiles.*) And you know what?
I don't think she did . . . I don't think she liked 'em at all. Not one
teeny bit . . . (*Beat.*) Funny how life works things out like that . . .
right there in front of you sometimes . . . isn't it? I think so. (*Beat.*)
Yeah. It's funny.

He stops talking for a moment. Looks at us. Nods. Looks away.

THE END.

woman - 30s

A WOMAN *in her thirties. Looking at us.*

WOMAN   . . . I saw an old boyfriend yesterday. It was probably—no,
that's not right. It was the day *before* yesterday. Two days ago
now. That's when I saw him. (*Beat.*) He was driving and we were
both stopped at a light and I was sitting there, I'm glancing down
at my phone—not texting or anything like that, I promise you
I wasn't, I try not to do that because it really is dangerous, terribly
dangerous, and I know a girl who died that way. Back in college.
Texting. She wasn't doing it but she was reading one that was
sent to her. Just going along in her little car . . . she had one of
those Mazda Miatas, which are so tiny . . . and she looked down
to check a text she received (this has all been verified by the
police) and she flipped her car on a bad turn about twenty miles
out of town. Right over on its hood, and that killed her instantly
. . . not certain if she had the top on or not but I'm not sure that
would've mattered—Karen had a soft convertible, not the hard
shell type so there wasn't really any hope for her after she did
that. She died. Because of a text that some guy she was going
with at the time sent to her. You know what it said? "I DON'T
KNOW." (*Beat.*) No, I'm not saying . . . I *do* know what it said,
I'm not being coy . . . it said those words: I DON'T KNOW. He

was responding to something she had written to him earlier in the day . . . like, four hours earlier when he was in class, and he was just answering her back right then, and he wrote: "I-DON'T-KNOW." The authorities tracked down on her phone what she'd asked him and it was a text she'd sent to him—they'd only been out maybe three times together, and she had texted him this: "SO, DO YOU LIKE ME OR NOT?" Karen had just put it out there . . . which was so like her . . . and asked the guy where they stood and that's what he wrote her back. The truth. I DON'T KNOW. (*Beat.*) Of course no one's sure if she ever read the thing . . . if she actually saw what he wrote to her . . . but she did receive it. She did *click* on it. So who knows? I've always wanted to believe she didn't read it . . . that she died just trying to hold her phone and drive and it was an accident that was stupid and should've been avoided but I don't know for sure. No one does. There's just too many other things that might be true if she did see that text . . . stuff that I don't want to be real or want to have happened, if in fact she actually knew how that guy felt. You know? Because Karen used to *really* fall hard for people—boys— and I don't know what she might've done if she put herself out there like that with someone and then they wrote back to her "I DON'T KNOW." I don't wanna believe that she would've . . . you know . . . but anything's possible and I also don't want to put that on *him*. That kind of guilt for having written what was proba-bly just the truth—the truth based on him and her and how long they'd been dating at that point—and who wants to carry that around for the rest of their life? Not him. I'm sure he wouldn't want to. Not me, either. (*Beat.*) But I suppose I do. A little . . . (*Beat.*) See, the reason he was unsure about whether he had any feelings for Karen was because at that same moment he was

dating another girl. *Me*. Obviously. I mean, obviously you've figured that out by now . . . or just did. And I knew that she liked him
and that meeting guys—or *keeping* guys, really, keeping them was
more specifically her problem—but I was young and I didn't really
care and I liked him so I just did that. I dated him, too, and so we
kept it a secret—from her, at least—and that was that. He sort've
had the best of both worlds there for a little while . . . being around
Karen, who was a nice person and had a cute car . . . plus some
kind of trust fund—maybe not that, maybe not something as elaborate as a "fund" but money of some kind, not just living off financial aid or student loans like the rest of us. She had all that so
he did, too . . . and he also had me. Someone on the side that he
could play with and be with and . . . just . . . whatever. The guy
was seeing both of us at the same time and I knew it and didn't
care and she didn't know a thing about it and so . . . that was the
story. He'd go back and forth with us, sometimes straight from
one of us to the other—and I mean, in the *same* night. But it
wasn't gross, it wasn't dirty . . . he had this *way* about him that
was just sort of boyish . . . likeable and tender and . . . God, funny
as well, he could really make you laugh . . . (*Beat.*) We both liked
him. At that point, and I mean at the beginning point, there wasn't
really any harm being done. Didn't seem like it to me, anyhow . . .
but yes, she *technically* met him first and so . . . should I not've
gone out with them for a meal on one occasion or talked to him
when we ran into each other on campus or that type of thing?
Maybe . . . maybe so. Isn't that what friends do—they're supposed to watch out for each other? But I didn't . . . I did not do
that and/or want to or even feel some nagging pain in my side
telling me there was something morally wrong with what was
happening. And there were others, too . . . we didn't know that,

at the time, Karen or me, but there were a few other girls that
he was involved with, too. A *few*. *Quite* a few. Which is not really
for me to judge, I don't think, and he was not the only guy that
I would go out with—or even *slept* with—during that semester,
either, but I think it was a much bigger deal for Karen. I feel like it
was for her, or would've been, if she'd known . . . (*Beat.*) Maybe
she *did* know. Maybe she did—maybe that's even why she sent
that text to him in the middle of a school day when she could've
just as easily talked to him that night . . . asked him flat out, to his
face. That's how *I* would've done it . . . I mean, if I'd cared. (*Beat.*)
I honestly don't know what was going on with her at that moment
or during that day so we're just speculating to think that there is
any validity to the idea that Karen may or may not've spun out of
control and crashed her car on purpose. The police couldn't say
and the coroner couldn't tell and none of her friends or family or
school officials felt like this was anything other than a tragedy that
was bound to happen to a young girl who was texting someone
while she was driving a sports car on a decidedly dangerous and
twisty road. And so that was that. She died that day, Karen did,
and no one's even felt the need to ask any questions or raise
their eyebrows or request further investigations into the case.
(*Beat.*) It was hard to go on, of *course*. I mean, not as a person—
I'm sorry . . . I made that sound very maudlin but that isn't what
I meant—of *course* I could go on with my life. Of course I could.
I had to . . . that's what you do. It just is. I mean him and me; as
a couple, or whatever it is we were—I never bothered to *text* him
to find out, never once—but that's who I mean. The two of us.
We had been sneaking around the whole time, really, ever since
we first decided to go see a movie together without her, without
Karen . . . and once she died . . . well . . . didn't seem like the right

time to suddenly come out as this big romantic partnership with him and so we kept going on—for a little while, at least—but it began to drop off like those things do, like this probably would've done anyway, even if such a bad thing hadn't happened. But it had and so it was doubly doomed, I think. Whatever it is we'd found in each other. He quit calling . . . or calling very often . . . and I did the same or one of us would go after the other for a week or so and then give up, date other people . . . it was not a big thing, really. Very normal and nice and doomed to failure, like most every love story you see in college or high school. That's just what happens. (*Beat.*) But that was him, sitting there at the light. Next to me in his car . . . nearly ten years later and in a different *state* even. Just by a fluke of coincidence were we ever there together, even just for these few little seconds. (*Beat.*) I started to roll down my window, to wave to him . . . but I didn't. I let it go. What would I say to him? Make him pull over or follow me to a Denny's and have a meal together, talking about old times and all that? See who is now married or has kids or doesn't and why? Or sleep together even—I was in town on business so he might be, too—but what would be the point of that? None. There would not be one . . . except for the act of doing it. Proving to ourselves that we're still here. Still around. *Alive.* So I drove off. Turned my head and drove away. (*Beat.*) . . . And that's the end of the story.

She stops talking for a moment. Looks at us. Nods. Looks away.

THE END.

man - 40s

A MAN in his forties. Looking at us.

MAN . . . I love this game. I do. That's one thing you should know
about me, before we get all . . . I do love it. I really do. Not that
I don't get into football or, or other crap like that, some hockey,
whatever, but baseball is my game of choice, no question.
Without question. I'm a baseball guy, that's me. It is. (*Beat.*) I'm
also—not to, like, blow my own trumpet here or whatnot, but—
I've also coached a little. I have. Yep. I don't mean, you know,
not in a *professional* capacity or anything, at college, no, but just
for boys down at the . . . you know, whatdoyacallit? The Parks &
Rec Department. In the summer. I've been a batting coach with
one of the teams there since my oldest—Dale, Jr.—he went and
tried out one spring. Kid's a fantastic ballplayer, really is, walked
on and took over the shortstop position from a neighbor boy
who'd been playing for, like, three years previous, so . . . (*Beat.*)
And he can hit, too . . . *un*-believable power for a young guy and
this really great respect for the game. The rules and all that, you
know? A regular little sportsman-of-the-year and I wanted to be
a part of that so I started helping kids learn to bat at some of the
practices—holding the thing correctly, learning to swing through
the pitch, finding their stance, etc. No big deal, really, but it can

make a bit of a difference in somebody's career if a person like me takes an interest in them early on . . . helps instill the basics at the right age . . . you'd be surprised. Uh-huh. Lot of boys I've worked with have gone right on up through their school programs and been highly successful . . . including a few scholarships to various colleges, local anyway, and even one kid—played just after my son did—he's on a minor-league team in the Seattle area, could even end up with a major league franchise if he plays his cards right. And you know what? Still holds that bat exactly the way I showed him, over ten years ago. Yep. (*Beat.*) My kid, as good as he is, he ended up working construction and only plays on weekends in the summer, so, you know . . . but he knows I love 'em, no matter what he became, so yeah; still plays a hell of an infield game, even if it's just slow pitch over there at those public fields. I go see him play some evenings, last game of the night on a Saturday and it just . . . well, you know how it is when it's your own son. It's just . . . pleasing. (*Beat.*) You keep looking at me funny . . . you're thinking that I'm . . . I mean, you probably recognize me, right? Realize that I'm somebody you know from somewhere but can't put your finger on it yet. Isn't that it? Umm-hmm. Tell ya what, I'll give you a hint and you'll probably get it right away. Just like that. (*He snaps his fingers.*) Two years ago, Morgan Field. Wizards vs. the Bulldogs. You got it? No? Yes? I was the guy. You know . . . the *guy*, with the whole . . . it was on the news for, like, a week! The fight. The parents who . . . and we all got into that tussle and, you know? Yeah. That was *me*. (*Beat.*) Yep, *now* you remember, don't ya? Sure. It was a big deal around here . . . even made the national news for a couple days there. Our pictures. And still, to this day, I don't know how it got started, I really don't. I said *one* thing—one!—a tiny comment about the way this guy's

kid was crouching in the batter's box and, yes, okay, I made
a bit of a joke out of the thing—I mean, you probably never saw
any of the amateur video from that day but it's still available out
there, folks on the Internet and whatnot—but the kid had a bad
attitude. He was a terrible hitter from what I could see, it was
only like his *fourth* time at bat, and so I just yelled it out, no big
deal; that's half of the Little League experience . . . dealing with
the crowd. My boy did it, and he was an amazing player, but
people would still always be saying stuff, just crazy stuff, about
his name and his, I dunno, his *socks* and shit; the *point* was to try
and throw the kids off! That's the *idea* behind it . . . and this guy
goes ballistic in the crowd. From the visitor bleachers way over
there on the opposite side of the field this one comes running
over, charging straight at me . . . I can see what he's doing, and
he looks like he's, you know, like he's out of his head . . . swearing
and almost crying . . . he's red in the face and these, like, beads of
water (I don't know if they're tears) coming off him. A couple dads
down front try to stop him but he plows right over them—knocks
down a *mom* holding her baby even!—and he hits me like a . . .
like some *train* coming out of a tunnel. WHAM! Up over the stands
and down onto the metal seats, him swinging these wild punches
as I'm defending myself and screaming up into his face . . . choking
and hissing at him . . . with these people gathering behind him and
grabbing his neck but he's . . . he's not going anywhere, won't
give up . . . he's sitting on my chest, has me on my back now and
almost split in two—you know, like, dropped down there into the
floor section and no way I can get to my feet, my air's getting all
cut off—and him punching away at me. All I can see before I pass
out is that look in the guy's eyes as he's smashing my face. His
eyes are all . . . well, you just don't forget a thing like that. Not

ever. (*Beat.*) Anyway, that's how it started and I know it was stupid, just a stupid thing to say and to be involved in and all that but what're you gonna do? You can't take it back, you can't . . . and all the wishing and praying in the world won't make it okay again, make everything go back to zero and be alright. You're stuck with what you've done and you're gonna feel like shit about your part in it forever. Yeah, for all time . . . forever and ever. Or like the one guy said, in his poem there . . . with the bird? "Evermore." That's a long time to be sorry about one little dumb thing you did but that's the way it works and from then on, that *second*, that's your lot in life. To go walking around and feeling crappy about what you did and how things ended up and the like. Your part in it . . . and what happened to your life in the meantime because of it. (*Beat.*) I mean *look* at me. What a fucking tragedy this is, huh? I'm not kidding ya. Forty-four years old and I leave three kids and a wife behind. Beth's a homemaker, doesn't have an *associate's* degree even, and there's not enough insurance or benefits or any of that shit . . . because *I'm* invincible, right? *I'm* immortal and in the prime of my life and an *American* and what the hell's ever gonna happen to me? And then something does, and there you are. You're gone and they're left and that's what all these books . . . all these many religious books that babble about Heaven and Hell and what happens next . . . *that's* what they're going on and on about. In a second, some split second of time, you're just . . . gone. But, see, you're left to wander around like you're still here and look at all the people who love you crying and trying to figure out how to live now and there's not a thing in the world you can do . . . not one. Because no one can ever see you again but you gotta watch all the outcome of what you did. Family having to sell the house and that other guy going to jail for a while—I wasn't so bothered by that!—and your kids cringing every time somebody asks 'em about that day . . . *that* is what you leave behind. That's what you get for opening your big mouth about some man's child who, for a few minutes there, you forgot is loved by this guy and he'll do anything to make sure that boy grows up strong and happy and secure. *Any*-thing. And that's when you sit down somewhere, in this in-between place where you now find yourself and you get sick . . . actually physically sick wishing so hard that you could just go back, go back for a second is all, and keep your big mouth shut and watch the game and go get pizza after and fall asleep next to your family just one more time. Just once. But you can't, no, you can't ever do that again because you forgot it's a game . . . it's only a game and that's something that will haunt you forever and ever and ever . . . (*Beat.*) I know it's hard, believe, I know . . . with the mortgage and people out there driving like maniacs and that new dude at work who is making you crazy . . . it's *so* damn hard to remember to just relax and to lighten up and take those moments of pleasure that come to you. But do: take 'em and pull 'em close to your chest and just . . . you know . . . just squeeze the shit out of 'em because they are so goddamn precious . . . so try, okay? That's all I'm gonna say to you about it, is try. Just try. Try and hold you stupid fucking temper and just . . . you know . . . try. Because it's only a game. It really is. It's a game. That's all. (*Beat.*) A *game* . . .

He stops talking for a moment. Looks at us. Nods. Looks away.

THE END.

woman - 40s

A WOMAN *in her forties. Looking at us.*

WOMAN . . . I'm running away . . . I mean, what I've done and am
doing, effectively, would be considered "running away." Technically. (*Beat.*) I hope you don't judge me because of it . . . write
me off too quickly. I'm a good person, I am . . . most anybody
I know or who knows me will tell you that. That I'm a good, regular
person. "She's a very good person," that's what they would say,
whoever *they* are . . . (*Beat.*) Long suffering is what I'd say but
that's another story. Well, no, I suppose it's not . . . it's part of this
story, the reason that there's a story to tell in the first place . . . is
due to the other story . . . my first story . . . my earlier life. (*Beat.*)
I married a man who beat me. I didn't know this at the time or
I wouldn't have done it—married the guy—but we do things when
we're young and we sometimes don't even understand why; it's
enough to just do them and hope for the best . . . that's what we
do . . . we hope for the very best as we push blindly forward in life.
(*Beat.*) He didn't do it all the time . . . certainly not in the beginning
. . . when we were first married he was quite the gentleman and
life seemed to happen in the way I always imagined it might . . .
in the way that little girls are taught to believe it would happen for
them if they did their homework and listened to their parents and

chose a good and kind man to be with. I did that. I did all of the
things I was supposed to do and yet I ended up in a bad situation.
A really awful situation that didn't allow me to be safe or live my
life or anything like that . . . I was a prisoner to a man who had the
ability to change personalities—that is probably incorrect and not
what a real therapist or psychology-person would call it, but—
he seemed to change right before my eyes, almost at will, and
when all of the hitting started I just couldn't take it after a while.
I couldn't, and I don't think I was wrong to leave. To escape. It
really did come to that—it was like the kind of thing you read
about in a story-book or in newspaper accounts of people during
the war. I had to escape that life to find the new me, the real me,
but that old life always seems to be there, too. Behind me, only
a few steps behind . . . waiting to catch up to me. To bring me
down. (*Beat.*) I don't mean to make this sound . . . so . . . dramatic
or to create the wrong impression in your minds about my past.
There were some good times too, I'm sure . . . I can't remember
any for you right at this moment, but I'm sure I could if I thought
about it for a moment. (*Thinks.*) Disney! We went to Disney World
one summer—the one in Florida—and I liked that, but it was the
place, not who I was with that I enjoyed so much so that's not
exactly right . . . but I could . . . I'm sure I could come up with a
memory or two of my time with him that wasn't terrible. I'm sure
of it. (*Beat.*) I'd met a woman . . . and before I tell you about her,
you need to know that I wasn't looking, no matter if that's what it
appears to be or not, that was not how any of this happened. It is
not. I knew her from years ago—all the way back in high school,
actually—and I got an email from her by chance one year, just
really by complete chance as she was the one who was putting
together one of those reunions that they have every five or ten

years . . . awful things where you go and see how much everybody has aged and lie to yourself that you're looking so much
better than they are . . . and she sent me the mass email, same
thing that they give out to everyone. Her name is "Tess," by the
way. "Tess." Like the novel, only not as tragic. God, I hope not,
anyway . . . Tess sent that to me and the rest of my class and
I sent back a response. Just a quick "Thanks and hope you're
well!" sort of thing . . . thinking nothing of it, hadn't seen her in
years . . . and that started it. An email exchange between us—
and I mean over the course of several years—and I found out she
was living in the East and was with a woman now and so many
things, things that I never could've dreamed of when I think back
to our time together in high school—we were on the debate team
one year and I think she sat in front of me in a Chemisty class—
and after all of that, so many years of nothing and lost in my own
world, my own life of moderate misery . . . I met someone. Tess.
(*Beat.*) I'm not really happy going into our situation and talking
about all of that . . . many things happened. Yes, we've grown
close and had . . . but that did not make me leave my husband.
It did not . . . when I did finally go, after a particularly messy and
awful few months . . . I left to save my life, not to be with someone
else or to be . . . no. The truth is, I fled. Ran away because I was
afraid. In *fear* of my life, like so many other women are—find
themselves in that place at some point in their relationships . . .
(*Beat.*) Yes, I went to Tess and have been with her since that time,
but I could just have easily hidden away in some motel by the
roadside if I'd not known her and I would've—I would be there
still, cowering in a cheap bed each night, alone, and waiting for
a knock on the door if I hadn't had her in my life, but I did . . . and
I do . . . and that's where I am now. Safe and in another world . . .

away from the danger that haunted so much of my earlier life.
(*Beat.*) I love who I am now. The freedom with which I live each
day, spend each moment with this woman who has become my
savior and my lover and my friend. We walk down city streets and
hold hands and laugh and see movies and sleep next to each
other and there is a calm in me now that didn't exist before this.
A desire, too, that I never knew in my marriage—or with any man,
now that I think back on it—a "want" that bubbles up in me when
I see her face or hear her laugh. A "need" I never felt before this.
I'm sure many people, if they knew what had happened to us,
how our lives have come together, they would hate it. Hate us.
We both come from a very conservative part of the country . . .
quite rural and a little backwards . . . beautiful lakes and trees
and I suppose I'm happy to have grown up there but no, not the
most liberal of minds . . . but that is of no matter to me or Tess.
We are together and that's all that matters. We found each other
and this is the life we want to share. Without judgment. Without
any hatred. Just two people. Happy. Alive. In love. What could
possibly be wrong with that? (*Beat.*) Still, some nights I think
about him. My husband. Knowing that he's out there. We never
divorced . . . and I know that he won't give that to me . . . my
freedom . . . if he knew the situation that I'm in now . . . he just
wouldn't. Tess is alright with it and is willing to leave things just
how they are . . . but I do think about it. Some nights. With her
asleep next to me. I'll think about him . . . or see his face in a
crowd—the middle of Times Square and a thousand people
around me—I'll catch a glimpse of his face. Watching me. Waiting
to get near me again. (*Beat.*) I've changed my email account and
all the things that I can think of . . . ways that he might track me
down . . . one day I'll have to face this, talk to him, and who

knows? Maybe he has taken up with another woman, some younger woman who loves him for what he is and I would be happy for that—so happy for him and to be rid of him—but I am truly and genuinely frightened of this man and so far I haven't been able to bring myself to get in contact with him. It's been a year now—over that, actually, more like 18 months—and I can't do it. Not yet . . . but I will. I will do it, no matter what I feel because I want to be free of him, of that marriage, and free to marry Tess if I want to, if that's what we decide. My parents would disown me! God, I can't even imagine what that would be like . . . but I love this woman and this life with her. It's worth it, it is . . . I *promise* you that it is. (*Beat.*) Someday soon.

She stops talking for a moment. Looks at us. Nods. Looks away.

THE END.

man - 50s

A MAN *in his fifties. Looking at us.*

MAN . . . I'm in love. I am. That's the truth and I just wanted to put it out there, first thing, get it out of the way off the top. Just so you and everybody else knows it, in case you've heard something to the contrary. You shouldn't have, that is not what I mean, but I just wanted to say . . . from my *own* point of view . . . that I am in love. I am. (*Beat.*) It's been years now, this love thing, I have been with a woman for . . . God . . . it's almost 30 years . . . and I've never been happier than I am at this moment. I don't mean right now . . . as I'm talking to you . . . but this basic time in my life, this general moment. I think we've found a renewed sense of, I dunno, whatever it is . . . *vigor*, I suppose . . . vigor in our relationship and we're just at the best time that I can imagine us being in, after all those years. That's amazing, I think . . . especially when you read all the stories out there, celebrities, people of all ages and types who are packing it in or giving up on what they've got . . . just throwing in the towel on a lifetime or a few years, whatever, folks everywhere who are not willing to work at it a bit . . . to try and keep a thing going with someone. Makes me sad, you know? I read a thing in a magazine—maybe it was on the computer, I'll go on there every so often but not too much—and it said that the

divorce rate in America is as high as . . . or maybe it was higher
. . . maybe even higher . . . than the marriage rate. Is that even
possible? I'm not sure, but it was something along those lines . . .
and, I mean, even if that's wrong, even if it's just *close* . . . isn't it
a bit shocking to you? It was to me. It's kind of unbelievable,
I think. We just . . . we're too easy on ourselves; we give up. We
don't like how things are going, have a cross word with somebody
we supposedly "love" and that's it . . . we're packing our bags
and out the door. Cancel the gas and electric in both our names
and we're done with it. Moving on. (*Beat.*) See . . . I made what
I consider a commitment to someone—better OR worse, meaning
good times AND bad—and I don't just take off, first chance I get
because we disagree about something, the weather or politics or
we have a bad day at work and take it out on one another. That is
not the way this whole thing was set up, as some sort of casual
arrangement that we can forget about if and when it suits us. No.
That is not my understanding of what a marriage is . . . and to be
fair, it's harder and harder to know what it is now, what with people
being able to do it from all walks of life—yes, I mean gay people
when I say that—and I like gay people . . . I mean, "like" is a funny
word; I know a few, friends of friends or co-workers, I guess . . .
but whether I *like* them or not, I am around them all the time,
they're all over the place in this city . . . and we get along fine.
Very friendly and I have no issues with that . . . but I was raised
with a certain set of values, not that I hold everybody else to
them, I don't, I'm just saying I was brought up with them firmly
in place and, you know, all these newer laws and propositions
out there now are just making things confusing . . . to me at least.
I'm confused. That's me, though, and I'm just . . . I could never
love a man. Not like that, not in that way . . . the way that people

do when they love someone who is the same as they are. I mean, I love my father—I did, he's been gone for a while now, but—and my brothers . . . I had friends in the service who I would say I am terribly close with, the ones who are still living, anyway . . . but never once did I feel drawn to them in a *romantic* way . . . in a *sexual* way . . . that's never happened to me. I heard of it, along the way, a few guys who it was whispered about, who gave each other hand jobs or things like that—not fit for mixed company, really, but yes, you heard about it happening . . . but that's not *love.* Is it? That's being alone and scared and far from home. That is looking for some *comfort*, from anyone, in the moment . . . in the dark . . . that's not "Let's get a mortgage together and have babies and that kind of thing." I know that lots of these people do that now, they want to have children together, in some fashion, adopt, maybe, or use one of those . . . whatever-you-call 'ems to help you get pregnant . . . a *surrogate* or a *donor* or however they do that now . . . but all of that still feels quite far and away from what the idea of "marriage" was. Back in the beginning. Not Adam and Eve, I'm not saying this in some religious or narrow-minded way . . . just that the notion of a *real* marriage has been pushed so far to one side to make way for all these other sorts of arrangements—so far aside that I can hardly even recognize the thing any more . . . (*Beat.*) Not that we haven't had a few missteps in our lives, a moment or so where I thought, "Hey, we should let this thing go" or something like that . . . one or two fights that you figure would be the end of a lesser marriage, but you have to be strong, you have to be able to say "I'm sorry" or let that other per-son be sorry without rubbing her nose in it. You *have* to, if you're in it for the long run . . . and I am. I love this woman that I married and nothing is going to rip that apart. (*Beat.*) I have a friend, this guy I've known for years that I'll go out for a drink with some nights . . . my wife can't *stand* him . . . but that's not going to be the end of us. See what I mean? I found a text on her phone one time . . . from some number that I didn't recognize and it was nothing bad, just sort of *flirty* . . . didn't even ask her about it. In the end, I let it go . . . you HAVE to. You MUST, if you're at all interested in a lifetime of love. The ups and downs of loving one person. (*Beat.*) I see young people on the subway, holding hands, that look in their eyes . . . that doesn't last! That feeling. That way of almost being sick to your stomach if you can't be near someone . . . it goes away but it also deepens, if you let it. You get to a place that's *so* great . . . it's *so* comfortable and nice, a feeling that is *so* solid and filled with peace . . . *that's* what love is between a man and a woman, when it's working right . . . that is the kind of . . . *joy* . . . you can look forward to in a full-fledged relationship with a woman . . . not the type of thing that a lot of these other people are having in a gay relationship or when kids just go & decide to live together . . . that sort of a behavior cheapens what married people are experiencing, it belittles us and what we have done and given up to be with the one we love. I think so, anyway. I really do feel strongly about this . . . that it takes away from what we've achieved and yet it wants all the benefits of that union, all of the good times and the respect that we get as a solid married couple . . . I'm just saying . . . I think that's wrong. I think it feels like a cheat and a bad way forward for both parties concerned. Maybe there's another name that they could use rather than "marriage" and then people wouldn't get so upset about it. I don't know . . . (*Beat.*) All I *do* know is that I have this great thing going with the woman I love, I've never been happier and that's all I need to know. Just that. If people want to protest

and petition Congress and go out there and make asses of
themselves so they can get some health insurance, then okay.
I've said what I think and I will let it go now. Happy to. Believe me.
(*Beat.*) I'm surprising my wife this year with a cruise . . . it's one
of those kind where they have performers on it and I think you
basically mingle with them a lot of the time . . . it's got a number
of singers that we like—they do shows on the boat each night and
there are some dinners that they attend—I think it'll be a real treat
for her. She loves that sort of thing. Famous people. We're just a
very regular couple but my wife loves the idea of being around
those kind of folks. And I love that about *her* . . . the little quirks
that make her who she is and me who I am. We're normal people.
Down-to-earth and approachable. What a married couple *should*
be. That's us. (*Beat.*) Her and me.

He stops talking for a moment. Looks at us. Nods. Looks away.

THE END.

woman - 50s

A WOMAN *in her fifties. Looking at us.*

WOMAN . . . I can't imagine going on much longer. I really can't.
(*Beat.*) I'm tired of life, to be honest. At my age? This just feels like
. . . you know . . . I've done it . . . like I did this, the whole thing,
and I'm ready to call it quits. I am completely ready, whether you
wanna believe that or not. (*Beat.*) How much can one person do,
you know? Go through? It boggles my mind . . . because it's not
fair, obviously, it's not at all fairly dispersed, the amount of happiness or tragedy or however you want to call it that people face,
it's just not. I have friends—girls that I grew up with, from college,
yes, but I mean all the way back into childhood . . . who lead
these perfect little lives (a minor problem here or there, of course,
they're human) but no illnesses and no heartbreak and everyone
goes to camp in the summer so they take vacations with their
spouses and the family pets live on forever—these women just
seem to be blessed or lucky or something, and whatever they
are I'm not that and I'm just exhausted from it all. That's what
I'm saying to you here: I'm *exhausted*, I'm done, and I'm ready to
stop all this nonsense because it's time. It is. (*Beat.*) Look at me.
Honestly . . . *look.* Don't be kind or say things that you hope will
carry me on for another week or two . . . I'm past that. I don't

want it. Really "look" at me and you'll see it. People do. They do
. . . in the supermarket or at the gym, when I go for my workout
class, they can all just tell that I'm so over it now: life. I move at a
speed and with a shuffle to my walk that I look like a person that
troops have discovered after liberating a village during the war.
I'm *that* person, the one I've seen in footage on television, walking
around in the background of some scratchy black-and-white film
about the war in Europe. They would play things like that for us in
school . . . as a child . . . and you would laugh at that person, who
I've become . . . you would, you would laugh with your friends at
those sad little men and women who the camera would pass over
briefly and they would smile or wave or bumble off back toward
their shops as the jeeps passed by . . . I'm now one of *them.* That's
who I am. (*Beat.*) When did this happen? When did I become so
marginal . . . so forgettable? Invisible? I can't even remember
now when it started but it's here . . . it is . . . and I don't think
I can't take it too much longer . . . I mean, *why*? What for? To get
even more infirmed, to become even *more* pathetic and reliant
on my children or worse, on the government to take care of me?
That is not who I am . . . started out to be . . . I'm not sure I can
do that. Become that woman. Not even a woman, just a person
who is ageless, sexless. Useless. I was such a dreamer as a child!
My God . . . the girl in Sunday School who wanted the *most* out of
life, who loved things with such a deep and reverent sense of
desire—and as a woman in love, I mean, there was no one I knew
growing up who hungered for a man, for love, more deeper than
I did. Who was more excited to have children, to be able to work
and grow as a person and juggle my wants and needs and to be
filled up with this life. But now I'm . . . I'm just lost. That's what it
is. I'm lost. Like so many people out there. Searching the channels

on their TVs for something, any kind of sign that will say it's all still worth it, that life is worth living. I'm one of the masses who scour the paper and trawl the internet looking for a message, some tiny symbol that's been tucked away there, for my eyes only, one that'll make me want to carry on, limp forward for at least another hour or so. That's who I've become. That person. (*Beat.*) When you lose a child . . . it changes you. You're just not supposed to live longer than your kids. I firmly believe that. Sometimes you wanna *kill* 'em, when they're alive . . . but you're not meant to outlive them. It's a fact . . . I don't feel like elaborating too much, I think you know enough about what happened there for me to . . . I hope so, anyway. It's part of the reason that I've found myself unable to control what I eat or all that. Sleeping for long stretches during the day. Going on long walks in the park but cannot remember leaving my house. It's the grief . . . the pain you carry from your loss and it doesn't go away, it does not let up, not ever, not ever, not one day does it stop doing that. Hurting you . . . (*Beat.*) And that's just about my daughter. Just that one little chapter in my life of pain. I'm not complaining—you *know* I'm not doing that, I'm not that person—but I could go on. You want me to make a *list*? Seriously? Talk about what happened to my husband at work and him leaving me after, what, twenty-some years and how I had to face life after that . . . or what about the cancer? Should I get on a soapbox to remind everybody about that? Why should I? Who am I to say that I'm alone in all this, that I've had it the worst of all the people I know? But honestly, if you were to stack it all up . . . the misery I have had to deal with . . . end on end, I'm saying, up to the Heavens . . . I certainly wouldn't be in last place. I'll just say that and nothing more: I would not be a last-place finisher in the sweepstakes of humiliation and tragedy and loss. No, I would

not. (*Beat.*) Not that I haven't been blessed as well . . . I have and
I won't deny it. I was *born*, first of all. The miracle of life. God saw
fit to allow me here on Earth, I was born and raised and filled with
such joy and hope . . . as I mentioned to you before . . . but slowly,
so slowly I have been washed in the blood of human sadness and
death and disease and hate, and I'm not a negative person—I'm
sure you're laughing to yourself right now . . . thinking "If she's not
then I don't know who is!" but I'm really not—I want to go on, I do
and I would, if only there was a sign out there for me. A little lamp
that was filled with a flickering flame out on the horizon, calling
to me. Saying "Come this way, Dorothy, come over here . . ." and
I would follow that light to the ends of the Earth. I promise you
I would. Not too *fast*, not very *well* . . . but I would. (*Beat.*) But
nothing. For so long. So, so long . . . and I don't mean a man. I'm
sure you see me here and listen to what I'm saying and you think:
"She just wants to be loved." Well, ok, yes, that's fair. Who doesn't?
But I'm not talking in those terms—sexual or romantic terms—
this is not at all about that. I don't need a *man*; I need a *reason*.
To go on. To move one step further forward. Today. Right now.
I need that. (*Beat.*) Do you have any idea how many times I've
thought about killing myself? Just swimming out to sea or, or
maybe just—I don't live near the ocean so I've ruled that one out
for now—but taking pills or just stepping out into the street in
front of a bus or a car . . . hundreds of times. *Hundreds.* And
that's just this *month.* Honestly, I don't know what the *normal*
amount for that type of thought would be, suicidal thoughts, but
I must be well over any sort of a national average. I'm *sure* I am.
(*Beat.*) And so then you come along. You knock on my door and
you come in with a smile and some free literature for me to have
but what's that all about? I appreciate it, the company and the

gesture, but what's the *real* story . . . what are you *actually* offering me here? Do you know that just a few minutes ago—literally just before you rang my buzzer—I was rummaging in my medicine cabinet to see if I've still got any razor blades? That's what I was doing today. *So.* You tell me. What can you help me with or say to me that will change my mind and keep me from running a tub and slitting my wrists . . . the moment you walk out that door. Because you will. Everyone has, at some point in my life . . . everybody who ever meant anything to me has done it at some point . . . and so will you. Oh, you will, I know you will . . . you can smile at me now and reassure me and offer up the love of Christ and we'll have some tea and talk for a bit . . . but then you'll go. Back home. To your life. To the person you love and I'll still be here. In the dark. All alone. (*Beat.*) I'm not afraid to do this . . . I used to be . . . but I'm not any more. So tell me why not, why I shouldn't make it all stop . . . have the pain go away. *You* tell me. I'm listening. My ears are open and my heart is ready—so tell me. Go on. Go ahead. I'm right here . . . I am sitting *right* across from you and I am an open vessel so fill me up if you can. I'm ready and I'm waiting. I am. I really really *am.* (*Beat.*) It's all up to you now.

She stops talking for a moment. Looks at us. Nods. Looks away.

THE END.

man - 60s

A MAN *in his sixties. Looking at us.*

MAN . . . I see that Archie's in love. Again. You know "Archie," right? The kid from the comics? That guy? Of course you do. Everybody knows Archie. I'm not saying people still *read* him—I mean, some- one must or they wouldn't have it out there on the newsstand— but folks know who it is when you say that name. "Archie." It was a big deal back in the day . . . not so much when *I* was young, not then, but at least when my kids were growing up . . . or just in-between. Maybe around the time I got married but before we had the boys. I'm not sure now, and I'm certainly not gonna "google" it or whatever the hell it is you do on your phone. I hate that. *Smart* phone. Bullshit. Mine can barely make a call, let alone be a dictionary or . . . what's the other . . . an encyclopedia. Jesus, that's not what a phone is for . . . to do crap like that. It's not. It's a "phone." It's right there, in the name. "Phone." It's for phoning. Why everybody thinks this little gadget in their pocket has to be, like, capable of *moon landings* and shit like that . . . I don't know. I buy the cheapest, easiest one I can find . . . not even a camera in it, if I can help it. Nothing. Just a phone. That's all I need. To be able to *call* people, if and when it's necessary . . . like emergencies. Side of the road. Somebody hit their head on the ice. Things like that. You won't find me driving down a highway, steering with my *knee*, talking to my best friend or trying to figure out where the next Howard Johnson's is. That's not—doesn't matter. Just my point of view on things today. The way things are now. It's not worth discussing. (*Beat.*) Anyway, like I said before: Archie's got a girlfriend. Actually, I said that because I saw it with my own two eyes but I have no idea if he's always after girls these days . . . no idea whatsoever. I wouldn't be at all surprised if he'd been with a man by now. I'm serious. I wouldn't even bat an eye. In fact, some part of me feels like that has already happened . . . if not to him then one of the other characters who're in his stories. "Jughead," maybe. Seems like a likely candidate for "gay." That one was always a little bit fruity, with that crazy hat and his . . . you know what I'm saying! I'm not making things up here. Jughead was an oddball, no two ways about it. What kind of name is that, anyhow? "Jug-head." It even sounds sexual . . . (*Beat.*) Could be one of the other boys as well—who was there? I hardly remember—"Reggie," I think, or some name like that one . . . Reggie . . . or "Moose," maybe? Wasn't there a big kid, like, a football player named "Moose" in there, too? I think so. It's not surprising these days if a guy like Moose turns out to love boys . . . it's happening more and more out there in the world of sports. Almost every other week you hear about some person who's now got a boyfriend and whatever—swimmers and a lot of those types . . . *divers* . . . which makes some kind of sense, when you think about it—but football men and hockey players, too. It happens. So, yeah, could've been Moose that I read about or caught just a glimpse of, hanging in the magazine shop one time . . . but I do think they did some sort of storyline where one of the guys from that group—Archie's circle of pals—fell for another man.

That or it was some comic book that was drawn in almost the *exact* same way; like "we should sue you for stealing" kind of way . . . I swear it was "Archie" comics but not in a court of law. I'm sure, but I'm not *sure* sure. You understand? (*Beat.*) Might've been the other one. "Reggie." The dark-headed one. That guy was always . . . and again, this is me just reading over the shoulder of my kids or at the doctor's office, waiting to get a check-up . . . but that Reggie guy was always talking about girls and how he's dating so-and-so and gonna marry such-and-such and after a while, when things never work out for him and he's still going on and on about women, then it starts to look fishy. You know? Like maybe he's covering something up. I don't know. I'm just talking, but it's strange. I think, anyway. (*Beat.*) But not Archie . . . nope. More I think about it, I think he never would've experimented with another person. Not, like, a male person, anyway. This fella, this normal sort of teenager, with the red hair and the wide eyes, all the time doing this and that—fixing up his old jalopy or raising money to help somebody do some cool thing—Archie just keeps on going back and forth between the blonde girl and the dark one. "Betty" and "Veronica." Back and forth. One minute he has those hearts drawn in around his face and we know he loves Betty and then he's off trying to get the other one to go out with him. The beautiful one. Veronica. He can't make up his mind: one issue he's up and after the girl-next-door, which would be "Betty" (she's like the "Barbie" type) but not much later he's smitten with the other one. The real looker, I think. The brunette. "Veronica." That's how it was, all while I was aware of this guy . . . him and his comic exploits . . . but not so any more. No way. Not at all. I've seen it with my own two eyes. (*Beat.*) Archie is now seeing some Indian girl. He is. He absolutely is, It's on the cover of the latest issue . . .

or if not the last one, then the one just before that. And she is definitely an Indian—not the kind from here, not some American kind, not like the cowboy and indian type—but a girl from the *country* of India. Yeah. Type with the dot on her forehead. That kind. Uh-huh. (*Beat.*) And I'm not saying anything here—none of my business—and it's worth noting that the guy doesn't even really exist, I *know* that, but: wow. I'm surprised, I am. That's all. I mean: *Archie.* Not that there's anything wrong with it, I'm sure it's *progressive* and all that jazz . . . all I'm saying is that I was a little bit caught off guard as I'm in line there, eight in the morning with a pack of gum in my hand and just trying to get to work on time. (*Beat.*) It's like anything I guess . . . like I've been talking about . . . phones or Archie or, or . . . even a breakfast cereal or a brand of cookies. Look at Cheerios or Oreos. Stuff like that. For years and years they go along and make a name for themselves doing a thing, one thing that they do very well. Really really well and that's what makes them what they are. A *brand.* Something a person like me can count on. Wrigley's gum. Same pack since I don't know when. Spearmint? Green. Peppermint? White. Juicy Fruit? Yellow. All the time, same thing and it *works.* It does. The system just works and I'm happy chewing my gum and the Wrigley family's happy buying up baseball teams and every piece of real estate in the known world, from here to wherever . . . Catalina Island. Right? *That* is the way it works here in the United States. We thought it up, we figured it out . . . people have fought and died so it could happen that way . . . *I* served, yes I did . . . and that's the system. How things are. Then suddenly, middle of nowhere, some kid comes out of law school or one of those other places that I find really very suspect—the *Rhode Island School of Design*—and they've figured out a better way to make the mousetrap. Created some kind of new wheel that rolls better or a fuel that is less something or more of a whatnot . . . I don't know but you know what I'm saying and what I'm saying is true of a certain way we do things today. People: if it's not broke, don't fix it. You ever heard that one? Huh? Well, it's true . . . Not just a quote but the *truth*. Leave it alone. Leave things be. Don't need twelve kinds of Cheez-its and forty-five types of Doritos or, I mean, what about cars? Mercedes. They've ruined that company . . . don't care how much money they make . . . it used to be a classy car. *Classy*. Now it's got twenty different styles—the nice one and a cheap one and a little one—nothing means anything any longer. It's all just "stuff." Shapeless, similar stuff that is indistinguishable from any other stuff . . . ."stuff from other countries" stuff . . . and that is not America. It's not. We're the best. We're special, we are . . . and there's only one way to stay that way. You-don't-water-down-what-you-got. Food, cars. The clothes you buy. And people. I don't care if he's a comic or not . . . Archie can't go and marry some Indian girl! What's gonna come of that? Huh? Different customs and different *mores*. Religions. The children would be torn this way and that way—I'm sure they even burn their women after a man dies over there. They do. Right? I'm pretty sure that's true . . . and that's no way for the wife of Archie to end up. I mean, right? That's awful. Even for a *drawing*. (*Beat.*) Anyway, 'nuf said. I've said my piece and I'll say no more. It's no big deal to me . . . it's not. It really isn't. (*Beat.*) I'm just looking out for the guy. That's all . . .

He stops talking for a moment. Looks at us. Nods. Looks away.

THE END.

woman - 60s

A WOMAN *in her sixties. Looking at us.*

WOMAN . . . I . . . the thing is, I'm seeing someone now. That's the
nice thing, the best bit of this is that. I've met someone. (*Beat.*)
It's been a while . . . I don't want to say how long, not exactly, but
long enough as to make this special. Very special. *Quite* special,
really. Quite. He's one of the men from my French class—I've
been taking lessons over the past year and he's there at the
college with me, Monday nights—anyway, that's how we met. It
happened like that. We were seated next to each other and we
met. (*Beat.*) He's very handsome. Not some unrealistic sort of
handsome, not a "movie star" handsome or that kind of thing,
not like that . . . but quite good-looking. Certainly not average.
At all. No. People look at him—my classmates and other folks on
campus, during our coffee break—they see him and quite a few
heads turn in our direction. More than a few, actually. Many.
He's *that* striking . . . with his silver hair and a very rugged look;
like one of those men they used to have in the cigarette ads back
when those kind of things could be shown on billboards and in
magazines . . . that's what he reminds me of. A man like that.
  A nice-looking man with a cigarette in his hand. He doesn't
smoke—just to be clear, he's a non-smoker ever since his wife

passed away from cancer, a year and a half ago . . . she was older but still, it was the lung cancer that took her—but that's the way he *looks*. I just wanted to . . . am I making any kind of sense? I hope so. (*Beat.*) When I say I'm "seeing" him, I suppose that's a stretch of my own . . . whatever that would be . . . a wish or a hope . . . my *imagination*, I guess . . . but not completely. These thoughts are not completely without merit. No, they are not. Reason being, he recently asked me to accompany him on a trip, a kind of *weekend getaway* upstate that I'm—I don't think it's any secret to say this—I am actually contemplating quite seriously. Why shouldn't I? I mean, just because I happen to be a little older—and wiser as well, I'm definitely that—I don't see how come I can't run off and do something a bit impetuous as well, a bit daring in that way that younger people do. I don't see it as dangerous, as my son would, I just don't . . . if it's anything, then it's carefree . . . that's the term for it: carefree. I'm making a choice for me, something I want and probably need as well . . . I *need* some kind of adventure in my life and I feel like this is it. That this may be the thing that's calling out for me to do and I won't be sorry, I won't be . . . I'm sure of it. I just am. (*Beat.*) When I was younger . . . it must've been . . . oh, how long ago now . . . probably in my thirties or so . . . I could've been forty, even . . . if I was then I had just turned, right around my fortieth birthday . . . I met a man. A wonderful man. He was so lovely, and sweet to me . . . but I was married at the time, still "attached," as they say sometimes . . . I was *attached* . . . and I was not available for that kind of thing. For romance. (*Beat.*) He did kiss me . . . one time, just the once, at a party in the city—we were living up near White Plains when all this happened, had told ourselves that we needed to be out of New York to raise the kids— we had two children together, my husband and I . . . my son and

a beautiful daughter, Gabby—and I'm not sure . . . was it
New Year's? Might've been, something we were downtown for,
could've been an office party or whatnot . . . but obviously, yes,
I'd been drinking and it was late . . . it was some moment like that,
an event, where things get the better of you and so it happens.
A kiss. One single little kiss that I've never forgotten, to this day.
(*Beat.*) And I won't do that, try and know if the same thing ever
happened to my husband, if he knew or ever had a time where he
was put in the same situation . . . I don't care. I honestly do not.
Whatever went on between us—not this man and me, not that,
but with my husband and myself, that's what I'm saying—and
there were some awful times later in our lives where we fought
over everything . . . I mean, every little scrap of paper in every
shoebox that we ever tucked into the attic . . . but I'm not talking
about that. I'm talking about a kiss. A tiny moment of tenderness
that slipped under the radar . . . everybody else's radar, at least
. . . and landed at my feet. Or, well, my mouth I suppose . . . to be
more right . . . more truthful about it. On my very own lips. (*Beat.*)
On the ride back home that night . . . usually I would've worried
that my husband had had too many drinks and that we were going
to have an accident or be pulled over on the Sawmill Parkway—
practical matters that a wife can catch herself up in if she so
chooses—but not this time. I watched the lights of the cars that
were coming at us in the darkness, tiny streaks of bright . . . and
it was perfect. If I'd died right then, that very moment, I think that
I would've been content. Fulfilled. Some part of me would've been
terrified, no doubt, some realistic portion of me . . . worried about
the children and the bills and such practical matters as those . . .
but as a person, as a woman, I would've died completely full.
Filled up with love. (*Smiles.*) And I never even knew his name!

That man. Never . . . not even to this day. (*Beat.*) I suppose that
I could've tracked him down . . . found out if he was a partner at
my husband's firm or that type of thing—mind you, it wasn't like
it is now, today, when you can track down anyone in a minute or
two just by getting on the computer, it was nothing like that . . .
you could call someone or look in the phone book or even make
an inquiry—a letter to a business or some reliable person—but
life contained so much mystery in those days . . . so much more
than now . . . I miss that . . . (*Beat.*) But I never did any of that.
Tracked him down. Asked around. Did what I could to find this
man . . . I mean, for what? To kiss him again . . . to touch him or
things like that . . . to leave my family because of my feelings for
a person I didn't even know the name of? People didn't do that.
Not when I was young. Well, maybe they did . . . I don't know . . .
or in stories, but that's not what I did. I didn't do that. No. I kissed
that man and I went back to my life and I never told anyone about
it before now. Just so you know. That's what I did. That's what
you do . . . when you have children and a life and responsibilities.
(*Beat.*) And now so many years have passed, my husband is
gone—not just gone as in divorced but passed away, several
years ago now, a car accident (on the Sawmill Parkway)—and I'm
taking classes and living my life and doing my best to stay con-
nected to my children—not just them but their children as well—
and I'm about to go away with a man that I hardly know. Have had
a handful of cups of coffee with. The friends I've asked . . . told
this to . . . are mixed in how they feel about my decision. Some
are excited, some frown and ask questions . . . others take it upon
themselves to go online and check up on this man—so far he
seems to stand up to the deepest scrutiny, even a criminal check
that someone (whom I won't mention here) from my women's

bible study did as a "favor" to me. He has a clean bill of health—much to the chagrin of my many friends and neighbors—and I plan to go away with him next weekend. He's picked a beautiful little bed & breakfast near the Vermont border and I'm very excited about the whole thing . . . I really am . . . (*Beat.*) The only thing . . . and I probably shouldn't even mention it, but . . . I know that it won't be like it was before. In the past. That other man. From *my* past. I know that however wonderful our drive up will be, and however many delicious meals we have at their Michelin-rated restaurant there . . . no matter if we fall in love or find a kind of happiness that can come late in one's life . . . some kind of warmth and friendship and security . . . I'll never feel what I felt that night in Manhattan. In the arms of a man that I didn't know. Who kissed me like that moment between us was actually the end of the world. (*Beat.*) Although now that I think about it, maybe it was . . . maybe it honestly was. (*Beat.*) For me, at least . . .

She stops talking for a moment. Looks at us. Nods. Looks away.

THE END.

Short Plays

pick one

Pick One had its world premiere as part of "Theatre Uncut" at the Edinburgh Theatre Festival in August 2013 (followed by a run at the Young Vic in London in November 2013). It was directed by Hannah Price.

FAT GUY
THIN GUY
MEDIUM GUY

Gary Beadle, Phil Nicol and Thom Tuck played the three guys.

NOTE: A slash (/) indicates the point of overlap in interrupted dialogue.

Silence. Darkness.

Lights up on three middle-aged white guys. In suits.

They're sitting in comfortable chairs. Drinking and smoking and talking.

FAT GUY . . . pick one.

THIN GUY Really?

FAT GUY Sure. Go ahead.

THIN GUY You mean . . . just . . .

MEDIUM GUY Yeah. Seriously. Do it.

THIN GUY But . . .

FAT GUY It's okay. Nobody's listening . . . we aren't taking minutes or, like, *recording* this or something stupid like that . . . ! We've learned our lesson on that front!

MEDIUM GUY Fucking *Nixon*, right? What an idiot.

All three men laugh at this. They smoke. They drink.

FAT GUY Exactly! (*To* THIN GUY.) So?

THIN GUY Ummmmmmmmm . . .

FAT GUY It's alright. Nobody is judging you. No one is gonna even know what you said . . . this is just between us. For now.

MEDIUM GUY Among friends. That's all./ Colleagues.

THIN GUY Okay./ Right.

MEDIUM GUY Something's gotta happen! The country's in a bad way and we're just talking . . .

FAT GUY Speculating . . .

MEDIUM GUY *Imagining* . . .

THIN GUY No, I get it . . . I get that.

MEDIUM GUY Cool.

FAT GUY Great.

MEDIUM GUY *So* . . . ?

THIN GUY Ahhhhh . . . I guess I'd say . . . / Ummmmmmm . . .

MEDIUM GUY Come *on*, man!/ You're killing us here!

FAT GUY Just pick one! (*Beat.*) Go for it!

THIN GUY Ok, ok! God, you guys are the worst . . . (*Smiles.*) I guess "black people." I mean, if I have to pick just one.

FAT GUY Blacks?

THIN GUY Yeah.

FAT GUY *Really?*/ Jeez! *Ambitious!*

THIN GUY I mean . . . / I guess . . .

MEDIUM GUY Don't look at *me*! This is your choice . . .

THIN GUY I'm just . . . yeah, I'd pick black people if I had to choose one group.

MEDIUM GUY That's who you'd chose to get rid of? Off the streets of America? (*Beat.*) I mean, if we could actually swing it, I'm saying?

THIN GUY Yep.

FAT GUY Totally gone?

THIN GUY Yeah. I guess. (*Beat.*) They kinda bug me. And they smell, too. A *lot* of 'em do . . .

MEDIUM GUY Interesting . . .

FAT GUY Very . . .

THIN GUY Is that the *wrong* answer?

FAT GUY No! God, not at all . . . it's a bold choice. I like it.

MEDIUM GUY Me too. Very bold. A super strong choice.

THIN GUY I mean . . . we're just *talking* here . . . right? This is just . . . us . . .

MEDIUM GUY Yeah. "Talking."

FAT GUY That's all. (*Beat.*) We're "talking."

MEDIUM GUY Yeah.

FAT GUY Of course.

MEDIUM GUY I mean, it's not like we could get everybody to vote with us on a bill like that! Hell, we can barely get people to show up on time, let alone talk them into a thing of this kind . . . so yeah, we're just *talking*. (*Beat.*) A friendly *chat*.

The FAT GUY *and the* MEDIUM GUY *glance at each other.*

THIN GUY Ok, cool. That's . . . great. (*Beat.*) And who would you guys pick? I'm just curious . . .

FAT GUY Oh. Ahhhh . . . (*Beat.*) I'd take the Asians.

THIN GUY Yeah?

FAT GUY Yep. There's less of 'em and just . . . they don't seem to make much of a fuss about things, so . . . I just figured . . .

THIN GUY Huh. (*To* MEDIUM GUY) And you?

MEDIUM GUY I'd go with Mexicans. Spaniards./ *Latins*. That type . . .

THIN GUY Oh./ Got it.

MEDIUM GUY Yeah . . . they're probably a little bit easier to deal with, I mean, overall . . . but they're a growing concern and I just figured we should get rid of 'em all at one time *if* the chance presented itself./ Right?

THIN GUY . . . I suppose. . . / Yeah . . .

FAT GUY I mean, we're never gonna capture that vote! I think the last election proved that, so . . . you know. Better safe than sorry.

MEDIUM GUY Exactly./ Don't ya think?

THIN GUY Huh./ Yeah . . . that makes sense . . .

The FAT GUY *slaps the* MEDIUM GUY *on the back as he talks to the* THIN GUY:

FAT GUY Originally he picked "women" but I had to remind him that . . .

while annoying . . . women aren't actually a "race" (*To the* MEDIUM GUY) They're a "gender," not a "race!"

MEDIUM GUY "Race!" "Gender!" Come on, that shit gets confusing after a while . . .

The three men laugh at this. They drink. They smoke.

FAT GUY (*To* THIN GUY) But I love that you just *went* for it!/ Right for the jugular with the "black people" thing. That's awesome.

THIN GUY Thanks./ *Well* . . .

MEDIUM GUY Yeah, that's great. Very brave.

THIN GUY I just think . . . you know . . . in these tough economic times . . . if you got rid of the blacks you're talking about a *lot* more stuff out there for everybody . . . I mean, there's no question about it. Right?

MEDIUM GUY Absolutely.

FAT GUY None at all.

THIN GUY With welfare and the, you know . . . social security checks and money that goes to whatever . . . free clinics and all the . . . / State housing programs . . . right?

FAT GUY Yes!/ God yes!

THIN GUY There would just be more *stuff* for everybody out there if they weren't around . . .

FAT GUY But you mean . . . like . . . dead? Right?

THIN GUY Well . . . yeah . . . / Right . . .

FAT GUY Because we already asked them if they'd go back to Africa . . . / I *know* we did . . . we did that years ago . . . like, back in Civil War times!

MEDIUM GUY And they said "no." They said "no thank you"' and they decided to stay here and move North . . . (*Pointing.*) They moved up North and shit happened. Bad shit. Look at Detroit . . . / Exactly.

FAT GUY A *lot* of those cities like that./ Chicago and Cincinnati and, and . . . *Philadelphia* . . .

MEDIUM GUY Really bad shit happening in those spots. Some bad, *bad* shit . . .

FAT GUY Places where black people live./ *Cities.*

THIN GUY Yep./ That's true.

FAT GUY Of course it's true . . . we're not making this up! We're not being *vindictive* or anything . . . God no!

MEDIUM GUY These are facts. That's all. *Facts.*

FAT GUY Black people are users and that's just . . . if you "use" long enough . . . for a really long time and lots of you are doing it . . . then you just run out of things. Right? Whatever things that people are using, that's what you run out of. Milk or tea or cars . . . *oxygen*, even . . . and that's what we're now in danger of, because of those people. Not just black people but mostly them . . . them and people like them . . . people with a "black" mentality . . . because of them we're almost out of things for us. Us and other people of our *ilk*. White people . . . the "providers." We are *providers* and we are ruining out of stuff because of them. The *users.*

MEDIUM GUY And that's *bad.* (*To* THIN GUY) I mean . . . you can see that, right? Can't you?/ That it's bad?

THIN GUY I mean, yeah./ Sure. (*Beat.*) That's *why* I brought 'em up. In the first place.

MEDIUM GUY Exactly!

FAT GUY We figured as much.

MEDIUM GUY But . . . you know . . .

FAT GUY You just can't be sure today. Unless you ask and that's always dangerous . . .

THIN GUY No, I get that . . . / It makes sense . . .

FAT GUY Good./ I'm glad.

MEDIUM GUY Great. That's really good news . . .

The FAT GUY *and the* MEDIUM GUY *look at each other again. Just for a moment, then back to the* THIN GUY. *They drink. They smoke.*

FAT GUY And . . . again, we are just *brainstorming* here . . . but lemme just . . . if we thought that we could do that . . . I mean, if we felt like we could get people to back us on this and help us out . . . like most of the American people . . . would you be willing to throw you weight behind us and support this?/ I mean publicly?

THIN GUY Oh./ . . . *ummmmmmmm* . . .

FAT GUY Just in theory! In "theory" is all I'm asking right now . . .

THIN GUY I mean . . . if you *actually* thought it had a chance of catching on . . .

MEDIUM GUY All we can do is *ask*, right? Ask people if they like the idea or not . . .

FAT GUY Honestly, I think that most people, most decent white people, can think of a black person or two that they'd be ready to get rid of . . . I'm saying if you made it *really* easy . . . like one-two-three./ (*Snapping his fingers.*) Like *that.*

MEDIUM GUY Probably./ I mean, I know *I* can.

FAT GUY Sure. Anybody could. (*Thinks.*) Oprah. Kobe Bryant./ That guy from Harvard . . . with the gap right here, in his teeth . . .

THIN GUY Sure./ Oh, I *hate* that guy!/ *Yes!*

FAT GUY See?/ It's easy if you start putting your mind to it . . .

MEDIUM GUY Rhianna. Kanye West. (*Beat.*) *Will Smith.*

The FAT GUY *and the* THIN GUY *look over at the* MEDIUM GUY.

Ok, ok . . . maybe not Will Smith . . .

THIN GUY No, he's kinda cool./ My kids like him.

FAT GUY Yeah, he seems like a nice guy./ Maybe we could let him escape or something . . . we'll just rough him up or whatnot.

THIN GUY Give 'em a *head-start* or whatever . . .

FAT GUY Yeah, I'd be ok with that./ Alright.

THIN GUY Me too./ Good.

MEDIUM GUY Fine. (*Beat.*) Not Will Smith. I'll write that down . . .
(*Gets out a pad and a pen and makes a note.*) "No-Will-Smith."

THIN GUY But the rest of 'em . . . you'd just . . . what?

FAT GUY We'd kill 'em. Just hunt 'em down and . . . you know . . .
(*Indicates motion of using a club on someone.*) Like they used to
do. In the old days. (*Beat.*) Or how they still do . . . with baby seals
and shit.

MEDIUM GUY Or . . . whatever you wanted . . . right? I mean, you'd
want to give people a chance to do it in their own way . . . however
they felt it was best. (*Beat.*) Wouldn't you?/ Just saying . . . some
people like guns.

FAT GUY Ummmm . . . / Yeah. (*Thinking.*) That's true.

MEDIUM GUY And we wouldn't be asking every person to do it, either,
right? U.S. population is, like . . . almost 75% white whereas negroes
make up only about . . . what? God, maybe 15, 16% of the total . . .
isn't that right?

FAT GUY I think so . . .

THIN GUY *Really?*

FAT GUY Yeah./ Something like that. Around there.

THIN GUY Huh./ God . . . it always seems like there's *so* many of
them around . . . but maybe that's just because I've been trying to
ride the subway more . . .

MEDIUM GUY Honestly, it's only about that many . . . so you really
wouldn't have to ask all the whites living here to do anything but
look the other way . . .

The THIN MAN *takes in this information and nods his head thoughtfully.*
Takes a sip of his drink.

FAT GUY Exactly! We could pick a day . . . maybe a Saturday or a Sunday . . . weekends are a nice time, more people are off work . . . and only like a *fifth* of white people, white Americans, would need to do it. Get their hands dirty. The rest of us could gather in parks or at baseball stadiums and, you know . . . wait for the outcome . . .

MEDIUM GUY There'd probably be a lot of killing at baseball stadiums, though, with all the black guys on teams . . . / And the *fans* . . .

FAT GUY That's true./ Damn. (*Thinking.*) Hockey rinks, then! Black people hate hockey.

MEDIUM GUY Yeah, that's good! Hockey rinks would be perfect . . .

They nod quietly at each other again, happy with this decision. They turn and look at the THIN GUY. *They drink. They smoke.*

FAT GUY So?

MEDIUM GUY You in?

FAT GUY We've gotta do something . . . this country is too great to just fade away and let's be honest . . . I mean, we were here first . . .

MEDIUM GUY That's true. (*To* THIN GUY) Right?

THIN GUY Well . . . I mean . . . the Indians . . . / Or *Native Americans*, really . . . but . . .

MEDIUM GUY Ok, listen . . . / If you wanna split hairs, then fine. Whatever.

THIN GUY I have a *reservation* in my district so I'm aware of the . . . I'm just saying . . .

MEDIUM GUY Then say it. What?/ (*Louder.*) WHAT?

THIN GUY I just . . . / You think we can pull it off? Like, *actually* do this?

MEDIUM GUY We think so. We've done some silent polling on the side . . . very hush-hush . . . *very* preliminary . . .

FAT GUY Obviously.

THIN GUY *Obviously* . . .

FAT GUY We got back some surprising numbers. Most people—the way things are today—it's a very popular idea. Us getting rid of at *least* one or two other races . . .

MEDIUM GUY It's *very* popular./ Yep.

FAT GUY Really quite popular./ You'd be shocked.

MEDIUM GUY And I'm not just talking in the South . . . or with old people . . . I'm saying college kids and some pretty liberal types, too. People who've lost jobs and, you know . . . just some pretty angry people. People who are looking for a change.

FAT GUY A *big* change./ A *real* statement.

THIN GUY Huh./ Wow.

FAT GUY Yep.

THIN GUY Well, this'd be *quite* a statement . . . I'll say that for it . . . !

FAT GUY I mean . . . *that's* the idea, right?!

THIN GUY True. That's true. (Beat.) I have this intern. Nice kid./ *Mixed* race, I think, so she's not, like, a full-on black . . .

MEDIUM GUY Alright . . ./ . . . uh-huh . . .

The FAT GUY *and the* MEDIUM GUY *shift forward in their seats, waiting to hear what this is all about. The* THIN GUY *clears his throat. Gestures in the air.*

THIN GUY So . . . would it be possible . . . *if* I agree to help push this through with folks . . . could I give her a heads-up, too? Just maybe a *day* or something . . .

MEDIUM GUY . . . I mean . . .

FAT GUY (*To* MEDIUM GUY) Yeah . . . we can probably make that work. If you throw your weight behind this . . . your weight *and* your resources . . .

THIN GUY Ok, great. I can do that. (*Beat.*) So . . . we're really *talking* about doing this? I mean . . .

FAT GUY Sure seems like it. Doesn't it?

MEDIUM GUY I think so . . . if you're in . . .

THIN GUY Ummmmmm . . . and it'll be discreet, right? Not just, like . . . *chaos* and these . . . big piles of bodies in the streets. I hope.

MEDIUM GUY No!

FAT GUY Hell *no*!

The FAT GUY *waves this idea off with a flick of his hand. Shakes his head "no!"*

MEDIUM GUY "Bodies in the streets!" God, that's . . . we'll make it fun!/ It'll be a big deal and lots of . . . *balloons* and stuff . . .

FAT GUY Bar-b-ques and, and . . . parades and good things like that!/ Things that Americans like . . .

MEDIUM GUY It'll be nice. Trust me.

FAT GUY And the next day . . . after we do this one little thing . . . there is gonna be so much more money and resources and just, like, *room* on buses . . .

MEDIUM GUY Good, affordable housing for people . . .

FAT GUY More spots open at colleges . . . slots we have been giving up for years because of Affirmative Action and bullshit like that and it'll all be over . . . in a day . . . a few *hours* of bloodshed and BAM!! Done. (*Beat.*) That's worth it . . . right?/ RIGHT?

THIN GUY I mean . . . / Yeah. (*Thinking.*) Yes, it is. I think it would be . . .

FAT GUY Fantastic!

MEDIUM GUY We *knew* you'd understand!

THIN GUY When you put it like that, it's . . . yeah. (*Beat.*) 'Cause we've never really gotten along, have we? Blacks and us? I mean, not completely . . .

MEDIUM GUY Not really.

FAT GUY No. Not entirely. I don't think so.

THIN GUY And it's hard, because you reach out to 'em and sometimes they're nice, but . . . a lot of the time they just have that *look* in their eyes . . . you know which one mean? (*Gesturing.*) That . . .

FAT GUY Yeah. Of course./ The "look."

THIN GUY Sure./ That *one* look . . .

MEDIUM GUY That "I'd-love-to-kill-you-if-I-could-get-away-with-it" look . . . ?/ *That* one?

THIN GUY Exactly!/ *That's* the look I mean. Yes.

MEDIUM GUY Right! So . . . *we* should do it first, don't you think? Before they stumble onto the same idea and start making spears . . .

FAT GUY It makes sense to me.

THIN GUY Yeah. That does make sense.

The men smile and shake hands. They drink. They smoke.

Great. So how do we . . . ?

MEDIUM GUY We'll send around an email blast, I think . . . initially, anyway . . .

THIN GUY Nice.

MEDIUM GUY Make some phone calls./ Very grass-roots.

THIN GUY Cool./ Great.

FAT GUY We should probably set a date, though.

THIN GUY One of you guys have a calendar . . . .?

FAT GUY I have one in my office. We can go take a look after lunch. Anybody starving? *I* am!

MEDIUM GUY Me, too . . .

THIN GUY Fine. Let's eat.

MEDIUM GUY Sounds good.

FAT GUY I'm never gonna say "no" to a meal . . .

The three men stand and start to move off. Still talking:

MEDIUM GUY Where do you guys wanna go?

FAT GUY I'm happy anywhere.

THIN GUY Yeah, me too . . .

FAT GUY So name a place, then./ Pick one.

MEDIUM GUY Go ahead./ No, you.

FAT GUY You.

MEDIUM GUY *You*!

FAT GUY Just . . .

MEDIUM GUY Seriously . . .

THIN GUY Come on, guys . . .

MEDIUM GUY It's up to *him* . . .

FAT GUY Why me?

MEDIUM GUY It's your turn!

FAT GUY No, it's yours . . .

MEDIUM GUY Just . . .

THIN GUY Come on!

The FAT GUY *stops, throws his arms up in the air. Shouts:*

FAT GUY Guys! *Pick* one! (*Beat.*) How we ever gonna get rid of black people if we can't even pick a *restaurant*! Huh?/ (*Grins.*) NOW COME ON! *PICK* ONE!

THIN GUY Fine!/ How 'bout *Cajun* . . . I like spicy.

FAT GUY Perfect! *Cajun* it is. (*To the others.*) See? That was easy . . .

And just like that, they're gone. An empty room.

Silence. Darkness.

the possible

The Possible had its world premiere as part of the "LaBute Short Play Festival" at the St. Louis Actors' Studio in St. Louis, MO, in July 2013. It was directed by Milton Zoth.

        ONE   Rachel Fenton
        TWO   Wendy Greenwood

NOTE: A slash (/) indicates the point of overlap in interrupted dialogue.

Silence. Darkness.

Two women are sitting in a living room. Staring at each other.

ONE . . . so.

TWO . . .

ONE Lemme understand this . . .

TWO Sure.

ONE Because it's a little bit . . . you know . . .

TWO I know.

ONE It's not what I expected you to say.

TWO I know it's not.

ONE I came here ready to be all . . . whatever. To *yell* at you . . . to
confront you . . .

TWO I get that. I understand. *But* . . .

ONE *But* now you're . . . I don't even know what to think about this.
What you just said.

TWO Think what you want. It's the truth.

ONE You're . . . (*Beat.*) *No.* It's not possible.

TWO You sure about that? You *sure*?

ONE I mean . . . that's . . . anything's *possible* . . . but why would you
do that? Seriously, *why*?

TWO Exactly why I said . . .

ONE . . . yeah, but . . . if you *really* wanted to . . .

TWO I'm not making shit up, okay? I'm not trying to get out of this, saying "You don't know what you're talking about . . . you're crazy if you think I'd ever try to sleep with your boyfriend" . . . I'm not saying that. At all. (*Beat.*) Am I?

ONE . . . no . . .

TWO Alright then. So?

ONE So . . . you . . . went after my boyfriend, like, *aggressively* after him for the last month or so . . . just so you could . . . then . . . what?

TWO You know.

ONE . . . *no* . . .

TWO You know *exactly* why. Yes, you do.

ONE For me?

TWO That's right.

ONE To get me. To *be* with me.

TWO Yes. I slept with your boyfriend so I could be with you . . . so that I would eventually end up with you.

ONE That's . . . no! NO!! That's ridiculous!

TWO Still . . . that was the plan. (*Beat.*) And here you are, by the way.

ONE No! I'm here to yell at you, to tell you to "Fuck off!" and stay out of our lives, *that's* why I'm here!!! Not for any other reason!!!

TWO We'll see . . .

ONE I am!! I'm here for *that*!!

TWO And where's your boyfriend?

ONE He's at work . . . he's . . . it doesn't *matter*!

TWO Does he know you're here?

ONE . . .

TWO Does he?

ONE No . . . I didn't . . . I found out about this and I . . . I mean, I *confronted* him and he denied it . . . said It never happened . . .

TWO But that's not true. Is it?

ONE I'm . . .

TWO Is-it?

ONE I don't know now. (*Beat.*) I don't know.

TWO What's that mean?

ONE It *means* he says he didn't do anything . . . that he barely knows you and would never hurt me or do that kind of thing to me, but then I come to you and you say the opposite . . . you say it *did* happen. (*Beat.*) *Several* times.

TWO That's right.

ONE So . . . I'm . . . I'm . . . I'm . . .

TWO But no, that's . . . I didn't just *say* it . . . did I? That's not completely true.

ONE No.

TWO No . . . I did more than that. I *showed* you that it happened . . . I gave you evidence that it did.

ONE Yes.

TWO Emails.

ONE Yes.

TWO And texts.

ONE Yes.

TWO Quite a few texts.

ONE Yes. That's . . .

TWO And more, too . . . didn't I? More than that.

ONE Yes.

TWO Just a few minutes ago. Right there . . . (*Pointing.*) On the coffee table.

ONE I guess you did. Yes.

WOMAN TWO *points at a small stack of papers on a table nearby. Offers one or two of them up again.*

TWO A hotel receipt. A hotel that I paid for but that he signed a room service ticket for at least twice . . . two different meals that we ate after having sex . . .

ONE Ok. Alright. *Yes.* (*Beat.*) Fine.

TWO So yeah . . . I think I did a little bit more than just "say" it happened.

WOMAN ONE *doesn't know how to respond.* WOMAN TWO *slides down to her and gets close. A hand on her knee.* WOMAN ONE *pulls away.*

ONE But . . . you're . . .

TWO What?

ONE I dunno! It doesn't even make sense! None of this makes any sense at all . . .

TWO It does to me . . .

ONE *How*? How does doing that . . . with him . . . make any sense if what you want—if you really do honestly want to be with me— how is this a normal way of going about that? I, I, I, I, I don't understand.

TWO Because you're with him. I needed to get you away from him. (*Beat.*) Simple.

ONE But then why would I ever want to be with you . . . the *person* who ruined that? Hmmmmm?

TWO True. (*Beat.*) That part was a risk . . .

ONE I don't even *like* women! I mean, as . . . you know . . . in relationships, I'm saying.

TWO That can change. (*Beat.*) It can.

ONE Yeah, no offense, but . . . I doubt it.

TWO "Doubt" is not "no." "Doubt" is not even close to "no."

ONE Then "no." I'm not a lesbian . . . I am not interested. *There.* (*Beat.*) NO.

TWO I'm not signing people up today, so don't worry about it. This isn't a *rally*.

ONE This is *so* frustrating! I mean . . . God!!

TWO All I care about is you . . . you being with me . . . I'm not here to *convert* you. (*Beat.*) We can "call" it whatever you want . . .

ONE I don't want to have *sex* with a woman! Shit, do you not understand what I just said to you . . .

TWO And . . . have you ever done that?

ONE What?

TWO Had sex. With a woman.

WOMAN ONE *pauses for a beat. Thinking. She finally says:*

ONE No.

TWO Never?

ONE No! (*Beat.*) I mean . . .

TWO What?

ONE Just . . . stop! Stop it! I'm really fucking *angry* at you right now, ok, so just . . .

TWO That doesn't mean you can't answer that. It's just a question.

ONE Once. In college. One time I . . . there was a girl in my dorm . . . she came on to me a few times.

TWO A few?

ONE Yes! A *few*. Over the course of a semester or, or . . . however long . . .

TWO I see.

ONE But we never did anything!

TWO No?

ONE No. I always . . . I stopped her. Before.

TWO Ok.

ONE Alright?

TWO Fine by me. (*Beat.*) *Right* before or, like, at the door? (*Beat.*) I'm just wondering . . . how long did you let her go before putting up a fight?

ONE STOP!

TWO I'm just asking . . .

ONE We never even kissed. Not once. So . . .

TWO So then how do you know?

ONE Know what?

TWO That you're not one.

ONE I'm *not*! I'm just not . . . I like men. I like . . . *that*. I'm straight or, you know, whatever you'd call that. I'm sure you guys've got a name for it . . .

TWO Who? Which "guys?"

ONE You guys! Lesbians. Lesbian women.

TWO I'm not a lesbian . . .

ONE Oh really? *No*? You're not?

TWO Nope.

ONE Okay, you know what . . . this is *too* . . .

TWO If I'm anything I'm Bi but I don't get into "labels" all that much . . . I hate to be seen as just one thing. Something you can stick a *post-it* on, so no . . . I don't really think of myself as anything but just "me."

ONE Fine.

TWO Fine or not, that's just who I am.

ONE Great, so, you go be the . . . *super liberal* . . . *polymorphic bi-girl* or whatever you are and I'm just gonna . . . I'll . . . just . . .

TWO What?

A momentary pause until WOMAN ONE *jumps up and shouts:*

ONE I'm *going*! I'm leaving now and I want you to stay the fuck away from my boyfriend!

TWO Got it. Ok. I got it.

ONE Yeah?! Well . . . I hope so!

WOMAN ONE *stands there waiting but* WOMAN TWO *does not engage with her. Finally she says:*

TWO You can leave any time you want to . . .

WOMAN ONE *is thinking, trying to decide her next move.*

ONE No! That's not . . . *no*!! You know what?! I'm not leaving until you apologize for . . . for all the shit you've done to me! To *us*!!

TWO "I apologize." (*Smiles.*) Better?

ONE . . . no.

TWO Then what else do you want me to say? "I won't do it again?" Something like that?

ONE I mean . . . yes! You won't . . . will you?

TWO I don't know yet.

ONE What does *that* mean?

TWO If I think it might help me . . . then yes.

ONE Help you what?

TWO Don't be coy.

ONE Just . . . stop, okay? Stop-that. (*Beat.*) I am not into women . . . I don't want that in my life . . . I don't want "you." Alright? Is it clear enough if I say it that way? (*Beat.*) Not interested. Not attracted. Not going to go there. WITH YOU.

TWO Maybe so.

ONE Oh my God!

TWO The problem is . . . you just said the *exact* same thing that your boyfriend said to me, first time we met up for coffee. (*Beat.*) Mind you, he didn't have to meet me . . . I called him, asked him to but he had absolutely no *actual* reason to do it. He spent the whole first evening telling me about all the reasons that we couldn't be together, every great thing about you and what he wanted to happen for you guys in the next couple years. All that crap. He said it to my face . . . he *slapped* his hand down on the table a few times. Everything you should do when you're in a relationship with a person. He did it all. (*Beat.*) Then I paid the check and he walked me home—again, didn't need to but he did—came up for a drink and then he fucked my brains out. A few times. (*Beat.*) Next visit or two he didn't say very much . . . in fact, nothing about you.

ONE Please don't tell me all this . . .

TWO I'm not doing it to hurt you. I'm just saying . . . as a *fact* . . . that because you look at me right now and tell me that there's no chance for the two of us . . . but you're still standing here while you say it, instead of throwing that drink in my face and *shouting* it at me from down the stairs . . . I somehow feel like I've still got a shot here. So forgive my apparent confidence but I need to go with my gut on this one . . .

WOMAN ONE *stands and starts to gather her things. Coat and purse and stuff like that.*

ONE Then I'll go. I'll get out of here . . . I'll take my stuff and just . . . go home.

TWO Alright. It was nice to see you.

ONE That's . . . (*Turns to her.*) Why *me*? I just don't even . . . out of *all* the people out there . . . people who would find you great and attractive and, and, and . . . why would you pick someone like me? (*Beat.*) Huh?

TWO You think I'm attractive?

ONE Agghhhh! You know what I *mean*! WHY?!

TWO Of course I know . . . but I'm interested in the other thing you just said . . .

ONE God, you know what? Forget it . . .

TWO No, come on. Just answer that. Answer it and I'll stop bugging you. I promise.

ONE What? (*Stops.*) Answer what?

TWO Do you find me attractive? At all?

ONE That's . . . not . . . who cares?! WHO FUCKING CARES RIGHT NOW?!!

TWO I do. *I* care. (*Beat.*) Isn't that obvious?

ONE You're . . . yes, obviously. You are a very pretty . . . whatever. A beautiful girl or, you know . . . I don't know! It doesn't at all matter what I think! (*Beat.*) You did an *awful* thing to me . . . to my boyfriend and me . . . and I'll never forgive you for that! *Ever*! So it doesn't really matter if I think you're good-looking or not . . . I couldn't never be with you now so what do your care if I like your face?!!

TWO Well . . .

ONE What? (*Beat.*) *What*?

TWO I just . . . people can forgive *so* much in life . . . like, I mean, really *horrific* stuff sometimes . . . things like rape or, you know, the Holocaust and shit like that . . . growing up *Catholic* . . . I do feel like it's possible . . .

ONE What is? Me forgiving you?

TWO I do, yeah. I think you could. Given enough time I do think so . . .

ONE Well, I don't *want* to . . . so . . .

TWO No, ok, maybe so, but that's different. I'm just saying . . . I think you *could*. If the right circumstances came along . . . if you realized that I'd actually done you a favor . . . then yeah . . . maybe you could.

ONE A "favor?" You think what you've done for me is a *favor*?
Splitting me up from a guy I really care about? That's a *good* thing?

TWO I think so, yeah . . .

ONE *Really*? You do?

TWO Yep . . . and so will you. In time. I really do believe that.

WOMAN TWO *looks at the other woman for a beat, then says:*

. . . are you gonna marry him? This guy of yours?

ONE What?!

TWO I'm just asking . . .

ONE That's none of your business!

TWO I didn't say it was . . . I just asked if you were going to . . .

ONE Maybe! Yeah, yeah . . . maybe I will . . .

TWO Which means . . .

ONE Which means 'maybe!' (*Beat.*) We've talked about it, yes we
have, but I don't know when or what month, anything like that . . .

TWO Even with what you know about him and me now? About what
we've done?

ONE I don't know! I-DON'T-KNOW! STOP IT!

TWO You know what? Maybe you were right . . . you should go now
because you're not ready to talk about this. It's too raw right now.

WOMAN TWO *walks away, leaving* WOMAN ONE *to stare at her from
behind. She finally says:*

ONE Oh, ok, now you don't wanna talk about it because I yelled at
you . . .

TWO No, I don't mind that. I kinda *liked* it, actually . . . gave me the
chills . . .

ONE Stop doing that! Stop talking to me like that!

TWO How? How am I talking to you?

ONE You know! You know what you're doing . . . in a *slinky* sort of way . . . with that sound in your voice and, and . . . these *insinuations* and this kind of . . . I don't know what it is but I do know what you're doing!

TWO Yeah? What's that?

ONE You're *seducing* me! That's what you are trying to do . . . you're seducing me! (*Beat.*) Aren't you?

TWO Am I?

ONE *See*?!

TWO What?

ONE Every question . . . you say another one . . . you answer *all* my questions with another question . . .

TWO Do I?

ONE YES!

TWO So?

ONE Just like that!

TWO Like what?

ONE Please . . . stop it . . .

TWO Why? Why should I stop? Do you want me to stop? I mean, really?

ONE Yes.

TWO You do?

ONE Yes. I do.

TWO Are you sure? I mean, one-hundred-percent-sure?

ONE . . .

WOMAN ONE *gives up for a moment.* WOMAN TWO *notices this.*

TWO See?

ONE What?

TWO That was "silence." That wasn't "I'm *one-hundred*-percent-sure."

ONE No . . . that's . . . *no.* I'm just confused.

TWO Really? Why?

ONE Because I came here to . . . to . . .

TWO I know, I know, you came here to *chastise* me . . . to say what an *awful* person I am . . .

ONE . . . yes . . . I mean, sort of . . . yes.

TWO And you've done that now. *So?*

ONE Yeah, but . . . I don't even think you care.

TWO Does that matter?

ONE I mean . . . it's always better if what you say to someone has an *impact* . . . that it *means* something . . .

TWO And it did. I heard you.

ONE Ok.

TWO I'm not saying it's going to change me . . . make me live my life differently, but . . .

ONE But you did hear me, right? *Correct?*

TWO Yes. I heard you. Loud and clear.

ONE Alright. (*Beat.*) Then . . .

TWO And me? Did you hear what I had to say to you?

ONE About what . . . ?

TWO You. Your boyfriend. Who you are.

ONE I mean . . .

TWO How many boyfriends have you had in the last . . . say . . . ten years? Since you started dating, even.

ONE I'm . . . look, I need to get home . . .

TWO Why? You can't even answer a question for me now? *One* question?

ONE Fine! I'm not sure . . . *actual* boyfriends? Or just . . . ?

TWO Yes. Slept with. Loved. Thought about in a long-term kind of arrangement way. That sort of guy.

ONE Maybe . . . like . . . five.

TWO . . .

ONE *Seven*. Or so.

TWO And how many of those ended?

ONE What?

TWO "Ended?" Like *finished* . . . at some point?

ONE Ummmmmmmmmm . . .

TWO I mean, *all*, right? All of your relationships ended . . . even this one, that you're in now . . . look what he's done. With me.

ONE So?

TWO So I'm saying it's going to end.

ONE No! No, it's not . . .

TWO Yes, it is. Maybe not because of this . . . maybe it'll take until after you marry and have kids . . . but it's going to end.

ONE You don't *know* that! (*Beat.*) You don't.

TWO I promise it will. I-PROMISE.

ONE That's . . . and so what? What if it does? What the hell does *that* prove?

TWO Something. About you.

ONE That's not even . . . what're you *saying*? If a person can't find happiness with someone of the opposite sex then they're . . . ?

TWO Maybe.

ONE That's ridiculous! That is *so* . . . come on! That's just . . . whatever. *Ridiculous*.

TWO Is it?

ONE Yes! I mean . . . what? Liz Taylor? Lesbian? Cary Grant? Gay? (*Beat.*) Okay, that might be a bad example . . . but . . .

TWO It's possible, that's what I'm saying. All I care about is the *possible* . . .

ONE If people don't stay in one relationship or . . . or find the *right* person . . . then that person is gay? Is that what you're trying to tell me here? I mean . . .

TWO I'm saying it's possible. I'm saying that it's highly possible— *probable*, even—the person we're talking about should take a really good, long look at themselves and see if they are who they think they are.

ONE You're just one of those people who *take* things . . . you want what you want when you want it and if you don't get it you ruin people. Families. Lives. You ruin stuff when you're not happy or can't have what you want or think you want! (*Beat.*) You want me. I say you can't have that and so you're willing to rub my nose in the fact that my boyfriend is weak, he's a shit, and like thousands of other guys who would sleep with a beautiful woman if given a chance. So what? SO-WHAT? I probably already knew that about him . . . I mean, of *course* I did . . . he's a guy . . . of course I did! Thank you for showing me exactly what I already feared and I already knew about men in general and my partner in particular! THANK YOU SO *SO* VERY MUCH!!

WOMAN TWO *goes to her and turns her around. Face to face.*

TWO So prove it then . . .

ONE What?

TWO Prove that you're not what I say you are. That you're not what I want you to be . . . that you aren't the person I've been looking for all of my life.

ONE . . .

TWO Because I think you are . . . I thought that the *minute* I saw you at that party last summer. You know what I'm talking about. The party. In the summer. You were there with *you-know-who* and I was there with you-don't-know-her—or *want* to know her, frankly—and we met going in and out of the house . . . I was going in to use their bathroom, you were just coming out . . . we passed in the doorway . . . at the very same moment . . .

ONE . . . the French doors . . .

TWO Yes. Those. (*Smiles.*) You remember.

ONE Yeah . . . we passed each other. We smiled.

TWO Exactly.

ONE We, we looked at each other and we . . . so *what?*

TWO You know what.

ONE No, I honestly *don't.* No.

TWO That's not true! You're not being honest!

ONE I am too!! I did not *feel* anything!! Not anything for you, anyway! It's not true!

TWO I don't believe you.

ONE Why?!

TWO Because it hit me like a thunderbolt. I'm a woman who has done a *lot* in my relatively short little lifetime . . . been with many people . . . seen many things . . . traveled the world a bit . . . and nothing has stopped me in my tracks like that smile from you . . . That tiny glance you gave me. Time froze. My life changed. Everything I've ever wanted or felt or needed—and I don't use a word like that one very often, *need*—all of it changed the moment, the very *second*, in fact, I met you . . . saw you. Became aware of your existence in this cold, crazy, terribly arbitrary but yes . . . occasionally beautiful world of ours . . .

ONE . . . stop . . . *please* . . .

TWO I think you could be everything to me . . . all that I can ever imagine in my life. I *have* to have you. HAVE-TO. (*Beat.*) Just so you know . . .

ONE I'm . . . not . . .

TWO I don't care what you're not. I want you to find out what you *are*. Who you *are*.

ONE You'll never know who I am . . . not *ever*. You can't. I won't let you.

TWO Yes, you will.

ONE No, I won't. *NO*.

TWO I already do./ I *know* you.

ONE No . . . / No, you don't.

TWO Yes, I do./ I do, too.

ONE No, you don't!/ YOU DON'T!

TWO Of course I do . . . / YES, I DO!

ONE You can't!/ You can't know me . . . who I am or what I want!! You're just saying what you want, that's all!! This is what YOU want!!/ It's all about *YOU*!!!

TWO Of course it is./ I want you, yes, I do! I want you! I WANT YOU! I WANT YOU! Have you ever really been wanted . . . *wanted* the way *I* want you?!/ No, I don't think so!!

ONE That's . . . / I don't know . . .

TWO You never have and you never will! NEVER, NEVER, NEVER! DON'T YOU UNDERSTAND THAT?!

ONE . . .

TWO This is *it*. This is everything . . .

WOMAN ONE *has nothing to say in return.* WOMAN TWO *speaks:*

One time.

ONE What?

TWO Kiss me one time. Touch me once. My face, my arm, my shoulder. Some part of me. Do that. Tell me you don't feel what I do . . . say that and I'll never bother you again. I will disappear from your life. Promise. (*Beat.*) I *promise*.

ONE That's . . . what'll that prove?

TWO That anything's possible. *Any*-thing.

ONE . . .

WOMAN TWO *moves closer to* WOMAN ONE. *Only inches apart now.*

TWO Dare you. (*Beat.*) I-dare-you.

ONE Once . . . ?

TWO Just once. (*Beat.*) Just one time . . .

WOMAN ONE *doesn't move.* WOMAN TWO *finally moves to her. Kisses her. Slowly at first but it builds. Finally they both pull away. Looking at each other.*

. . . *and*?

WOMAN ONE *stares long and hard into the eyes of* WOMAN TWO *before she softly says:*

ONE . . . don't rush me . . .

WOMAN TWO *smiles at this.* WOMAN ONE *moves closer to* WOMAN TWO *and they kiss again. It doesn't look like this will be ending any time soon.*

Silence. Darkness.

call back

Call Back (which began life as the short film *Denise*) had its world premiere at the Lucille Lortel Theatre (MCC) in New York City in June 2012 as part of a benefit collectively titled "The Heart of the Matter." It was directed by Carolyn Cantor.

HIM   Cheyenne Jackson
HER   Krysten Ritter

Silence. Darkness.

A casting office in a big city. Pretty quiet right now.

A GIRL *at a desk, fielding calls and running the place. A* FEW ACTORS *(*WOMEN *and* MEN*) seated on couches and chairs. Scanning over their sides for an audition.*

A LOVELY YOUNG WOMAN *off by herself. Reading a magazine.*

After a moment, A YOUNG MAN *plops down heavily near her. Smiles. Pulls a batch of pages out of a coat pocket.*

HIM (*Quietly.*) . . . what a life, huh? *Acting.*

Their eyes meet. She smiles, then glances away. He holds his gaze.

The guy smiles over at her. She nods. Finally, she speaks without looking back over.

HER . . . we've met before. By the way.

HIM I thought so.

HER I mean, in case you were wondering.

HIM No, I wasn't . . . I have a great memory and so I remember. That we have. *Met,* I mean.

HER Yeah?

HIM Definitely.

HER You do? You remember that?

HIM Of course! I mean . . . were we in something together? You seem very familiar . . . were you on that *Criminal Minds* episode I did?

HER Ummmmm . . . no . . . this was at an opening.

HIM Right, yes, right! We were at that one . . . *opening* . . . together. Absolutely.

HER Yeah? Does that ring a bell for you?

HIM Of course! We were . . . we had a *nice* talk.

HER . . . we did *talk* . . . yes . . .

HIM That *was* you! Right! I thought so . . .

GIRL *at the desk calls out a name and* A YOUNG WOMAN *gets up and moves over to her. A brief chat (unheard) and the actress heads off down a hallway.*

HER "Call backs."

HIM Absolutely! The *worst* . . .

HER I know. I hate 'em even more than the actual auditions, I think.

HIM Ha! Really?

She nods, turning back to the copy of Vogue *on her lap.*

HER Probably so. The competition's harder, you want it even more now 'cause you're close and then they keep you sitting and sitting and *sitting* . . . and most times, all for nothing! (*Beat.*) God, this business . . .

HIM That's so true! (*Beat.*) I love the script—material like this is *so* hard to find. To be a part of. I would *kill* for the chance at this . . . something on *cable*? Amazing.

They share a knowing smile as the desk GIRL *calls out another name—this time* A MAN *does the routine with her.*

Anyway . . ."hi." (*Beat.*) It's been a while.

HER   I know. I didn't think you remembered.

HIM   *Really?* Are you kidding me?

HER   Well, I mean, it kinda feels like it.

HIM   Not at all! (*Beat.*) I'm . . . I've thought about you a *few* times since then . . .

HER   What? *No.* Come on . . .

HIM   I have. Really.

HER   . . . that's not . . .

HIM   I have too! Yes! (*Smiles.*) I think you're terrific . . . so beautiful and, you know . . . *talented* . . . so of course I have. Sure.

HER   Well, that's . . . even if it's a *lie* that's very sweet.

HIM   It's not! I promise! (*Smiles.*) We gotta stick together, us actors . . . don't we? Need to trust each other a little bit.

HER   No question! All the folks out there who wanna bring us down, who we are as people and our work and . . . all that. Critics and *bloggers* and just . . . family, too, even . . . sometimes. (*Beat.*) The "haters," you know?

HIM   Yep.

HER   Or your boyfriend or even some guy you've sleep with— it *really* hurts when you give yourself to someone and you find out that you can't depend on 'em. At *all.* They say they'll stay in touch . . . that they'll call you back . . . but they don't.

HIM   So true. I mean . . . that is *so* true. Can't tell you how many times that's happened to me! *Dozens* of times . . .

HER   Huh. I'd love to hear . . .

The guy starts to say something but stops due to the GIRL *at the desk calling out another name.* ANOTHER GUY *up and off to the chopping block.*

. . . you were saying?

HIM What?

HER About the times you've been let down. I think you were gonna tell me about the different people who've screwed you over.

HIM That's . . . nah, forget it. Doesn't matter.

HER You didn't mean me, though, did you?

HIM *You*? No, God no! Why would I think that?

HER After everything we did that night. That night after the opening . . .

HIM . . . *right* . . .

HER Things I never tried before . . . positions I've never even *thought* of. I feel like lots of stuff happened that I can't even remember because I drank so much, or we took some kind of . . . I dunno. I just kept drinking and stuff . . . and then I woke up on the steps of my apartment building . . . which is weird.

HIM Huh. (*Beat.*) I don't remember that . . .

HER No?

HIM Uh-uh. Not at all. Not really.

HER So, then . . . what *do* you remember?

They stop as the GIRL *calls out another name and* ANOTHER ACTOR *goes up to the desk and then off down the hallway.*

HIM . . . you know . . .

HER No. Tell me. What?

HIM Us. At that, you know . . . the opening. *I invited* you to that event, didn't I? I remember now. I took you with me. (*Beat.*) I forwarded you my *e-vite* . . .

HER That's right.

HIM You had on this, like, pretty gown with the . . . it was kind of a . . . it was a really nice color as I think back on it—was it like peach? Or maybe *apricot*? Or was it more yellow? Not lemon, not as bright as that . . . but in that general world. (*Beat.*) Am I right? Was it yellow?

HER It was orange, actually. A pale orange.

HIM Right! That's right . . . I said "apricot" so obviously I . . . remember . . .

She studies him for a moment, then nods in agreement. She waits a beat, then says:

HER Uh-huh. And what else?

HIM What do you mean? (*Beat.*) Ahhh . . . you had *shoes* on, too, obviously, but I'm not sure what they looked like—and a handbag. I think.

HER No. I'm asking what else you can remember about our time together. (*Beat.*) Tell me.

HIM Oh. (*Beat.*) Ummmmmmm . . . more like us . . . you know, out at dinner—we went to that new spot over in Westwood, didn't we? I think so, anyway—and then we came back to my place and I played you a few of the old Jazz records that I collect . . .

HER . . . yeah, I remember that . . .

HIM Right? And then we . . . did we go out onto my deck? It seems like we might've . . .

HER We certainly did. Yes. Up to a *patio* . . .

HIM And then we . . . I mean, obviously . . . yes, we ended up in bed at some point . . . which was great. Lovely. *Really* special.

HER I thought so too. I mean, at the time...

HIM Me too! Absolutely so.

HER What with all the . . . positions and . . . the *promises* we made to each other. (*Beat.*) Plus, that *video* we did.

HIM Oh . . . sure, yes . . . the *video* . . .

HER . . . and then nothing. (*Beat.*) No-thing.

HIM No, that's . . . no, not nothing.

HER Pretty much, yeah. I mean, you certainly didn't call back. Not ever. *I* would've, I'd've been happy to call you but there was something about you couldn't give it out, your number, because it was a "work" phone . . . and . . . then we went back and forth about how you'd take mine instead . . . take it and text me a *different* number later where I could at least leave a message . . . (*Beat.*) It was pretty *elaborate.*

HIM . . . that's true . . . it's a *business* line . . . but I gave you my email, though. Didn't I?

Or . . . some . . .

HER Nope. Nothing.

HIM Wow. I didn't? I'm sure that I . . . was . . .

HER Apparently you dropped me off the next morning—this was after the opening of that last Harry Potter movie . . . not the second last part but the first last part. *That* one . . .

HIM I liked the first last part better.

HER And I know that you said you'd call . . . *promised* me you would. But you didn't.

The guy is about to defend himself when the GIRL *at the desk calls out another name.* ANOTHER PERSON *exits.*

. . . that's okay, Brad. That's alright . . . I get it. It's part of the "business." Getting used.

HIM Hey, no, that's not . . . I didn't *use* you!

HER No?

HIM Not at all! *Please!* (*Beat.*) If I forgot to call it's because . . . it wasn't at all about you . . . it was *me* . . . I take responsibility for it. It's because I wasn't able to . . . it just wasn't possible for me . . . at the time . . . to, you know . . .

HER . . . remember my name?

HIM Ha! (*Laughs.*) That's *not* what I was going to say. No.

HER But can you? (*Beat.*) *Brad*?

HIM What?

HER Even remember who I am.

HIM Yes! Of course! (*Beat.*) You were in that one . . . you did a soap, right? I remember that, and a *CSI: Miami*, too, I think . . . that girl with the . . . artificial arm who turned out to be . . . the killer . . . with a gun hidden inside of your . . . (*Miming.*)

HER My *name*, Brad. Do you know it?

HIM I mean . . . yeah, of course I do. *Yes.*

HER Ok. (*Beat.*) Ok, good, I believe you . . .

HIM Thanks. (*Beat.*) Listen, I didn't not call you because I didn't know your name!! It was because I lost your number. *That* was why.

HER Oh. You could've looked me up online, and we're also at the same agency. . . . I mean, in case you didn't remember that, either.

HIM No, ok, no, *that* I didn't remember, but the rest is . . . I really did misplace it. Your number. (*Beat.*) I thought I put it into my phone but when I looked it was—yeah, so I guess I didn't. Sorry.

HER How do you know?

HIM What do you mean?

HER If you don't know my name how can you be sure my number's not in there? (*Pointing.*) I mean . . .

HIM Stop! I *know* your name!

HER Then look me up and show me. Right now. (*Beat.*) Go ahead, *Brad*. *Show* me.

He begins to search in vain. Stalling a bit. Finally, she reaches over and takes his phone. He protests but he lets her do it. She scrolls through his address book.

Hmmm . . . lots of girls . . .

HIM There's guys, too.

HER Yeah, there are, but lots and *lots* of girls.

HIM . . . I get along with girls better . . .

HER Five "Amys" and six "Brittanys" and . . .

HIM . . . Brittany's a very popular name . . .

HER Oh wow . . . there must be about . . . must be almost ten "Christies." (*Points.*) Who is "Christie-Don't-Answer?"

HIM . . . she's just this person who . . . she went a little *nutso* on me after a few dates so I . . . just . . . added that little *code* . . .

She holds up the phone for him to see—pointing at the screen.

HER Ahh. And *me*. Right there. My email, too.

HIM That's it . . . I *knew* it started with a "D!" *Denise*! Of course I had it because I sent you the e-vite. (*Beat.*) Hello there. Yes.

She smiles at him, then drops the phone back in his lap.

HER Nope, wrong answer. *That* was a test. Try again.

He picks up his phone, looks at it. Puts it away. They sit for a moment in silence. Finally, he gives it a go.

HIM . . . look, I'm sorry if you're . . . (*Beat.*) So . . . should we run the lines? For the scene, I mean. Wanna run 'em together?

HER No, that's ok, Brad. It's the story of a girl who confronts a guy who's been a complete and total *asshole* to her. (*Beat.*) I know it by heart.

Before he can say anything else the GIRL *at the desk is at it again.*

Calls out a name ("Denise") and THE ACTRESS *stands up. She smiles at him and walks off.*

HIM   Wait, I thought you said . . . *see*?! I knew it was "Denise!" I *knew* that was you!

She stops and turns. Looks straight at him.

HER   By the way . . . I'm just here for a costume fitting. *I'm* already cast, so . . . (*Smiles.*) Good luck.

With that she is gone. Never looks back. The guy shakes his head and mutters softly to himself.

HIM   Shit. "Denise." I knew that was right!! "Denise." That's it . . . Denise.

He checks his phone. He sighs heavily and puts the phone away. The guy turns back to the pages in his lap. Looks around.

Checks out ANOTHER GIRL *who sits down next to him. Their eyes meet and he speaks:*

Acting. What a life, huh?

The girl nods but slides down a chair—one extra seat away from the guy. He notices this but lets it go. He goes back to memorizing his lines. Waiting.

Silence. Darkness.

good luck (in farsi)

Good Luck (In Farsi) had its world premiere at 59E59 Theatre in New York City in July 2013 as part of the "Summer Shorts" play festival series. It was directed by Neil LaBute.

> KATE   Gia Crovatin
> PAIGE   Elizabeth Masucci
> BREE   Molly Logan Chase

NOTE: A slash (/) indicates the point of overlap in interrupted dialogue.

Silence. Darkness.

A row of chairs. Stretching from one end of the room to the other.

One woman, seated. This is "KATE." She is digging through her purse ans belongings, looking for something. A bag of make-up. She is mouthing some words to herself and from time to time she glances at a small stack of pages on a chair next to her.

A casting assistant walks into the room with a clipboard and looks around. This is "BREE." KATE stands expectantly. BREE goes out and KATE sits back down. Begins running her lines out loud.

KATE   "... and now it's come to this, has it? The end of the of the road for you and me ..."

KATE hears something and looks up again. Sees someone coming.

KATE   ... oh shit. Fuck. Of *course.* (*Beat.*) I mean ... *really?* AAAAAAWWWWWW!!! FUCK!!

Another woman has entered and drops her stuff on a chair a few seats away. This is "PAIGE." She is some version of KATE, but dressed differently.

They smile at each other. Nod.

   Hi.

PAIGE   Hey there ...

Finally, PAIGE sits down in a chair and pulls some pages out of one of her bags. Starts reading.

KATE I should've known you'd be here . . . called in for this . . .

PAIGE Yeah. (*Shrugs.*) Well . . . you know . . .

KATE I mean, I *knew* I'd see you here. Second I read the sides I was, like, "God, if I don't see Paige Parsons there then some-thing weird is going on!"/ (*Beat.*) I go in for anything these days, a *tampon* commercial even, and BAM!!! There you are . . . on the sign-in sheet . . . / Yep.

PAIGE Ha!/ You *saw* that?/ I hate that I still have to go in for things . . . (*She looks over at* KATE.) I just mean . . . you know . . .

KATE No, no, I get it, of course! After your series and all that . . . I totally get it. (*Beat.*) Sucks that they cancelled it . . .

PAIGE Yep.

KATE After just . . . what? First season?/ Or not even . . . ?

PAIGE Ummmm . . . / We shot thirteen . . . but . . .

KATE Really? That many? I don't think I saw more than . . . I dunno . . . two or . . .

PAIGE Yeah, no, I think they only aired maybe *six*. Or so./ DVD has the whole thing . . . the *entire* . . .

KATE Huh./ Wow.

PAIGE Anyhow.

KATE Yeah. Oh, I'm "Kate," by the way . . .

PAIGE Hi.

KATE . . . hey. (*Beat.*) Anyway, good luck.

PAIGE Oh, thanks. (*Beat.*) Yeah, you too.

KATE *nods, smiles, then gets out some make-up and starts in on her face. Touch-ups. She finds a little mirror and her mascara. She begins to apply it.*

PAIGE *watches her for a beat, then speaks to* KATE *again:*

. . . I'm lousy with make-up. Always was. Ever since I was a kid . . . (*Beat.*) Adding a bit more, huh?

KATE Uh-huh. Just some *mascara*. I really wanna make my lashes "pop" for this . . . I think someone in the CIA would have *really* great make-up.

PAIGE Nice.

KATE Yep. I always do . . . brings out my eyes, which are, like . . . you know. One of my *best* features, I think.

PAIGE Definitely. You have *gorgeous* eyes.

KATE Thank you. (*Smiles.*) You too.

PAIGE Thanks. (*Beat.*) I mean, mine are ok. *Just* ok. Smaller. A little bit deeper set . . . They're fine. Guys seem to like 'em but, you know, they're guys . . . so they're not exactly *picky*!! (*She laughs.*) You're the one with the eyes . . . *trust* me. (*Beat.*) Anyway . . . good luck.

KATE Thanks. (*Beat.*) You too.

PAIGE *tries to work on her lines but after a moment she points at* KATE*'s mirror as she speaks to* KATE *yet again:*

PAIGE Hey . . . you think they *secretly* hold it against us?

KATE (*Looking up.*) What's that?

PAIGE That we're beautiful?

KATE I'm sorry?

PAIGE Nothing. I'm just curious, that's all.

KATE You mean . . . like . . . *who*?

PAIGE (*Indicating.*) Them. People. Everybody.

KATE . . . ummmmmm . . .

PAIGE Producers . . . other actors . . . out on the street. (*Beat.*) I know casting directors do . . . ! Those bitches *hate* us. Girls like you and me. *And* we're talented—which is probably extra annoying—I mean, I'm assuming you are. *I* am.

KATE That's so *funny* . . .

PAIGE Yeah, but it's "funny" because it's true! Right? (*Beat.*) Don't
you think?

KATE *thinks about this for a second, nods "no" and goes back to what
she's doing. She suddenly looks up and says:*

KATE I mean . . . God . . . I don't think so. (*Beat.*) Do you *really*?
(*Beat.*) I hope not!

PAIGE That would suck, right? If they did. Because that's . . . you
know. It just would. *Suck.*

KATE Totally.

PAIGE It's not *our* fault!

KATE Absolutely not.

PAIGE I didn't ask for this. To be pretty, or, or beautiful. Stunning.
Nobody *asked* me.

KATE Me either.

PAIGE We're just *born* this way. Right?

KATE I mean . . . yeah. Pretty much.

PAIGE It just happened! Parents get together, two good-looking
people and . . . sometimes not even that, not even attractive, it's
just some . . . combination of . . . whatever . . .

KATE Mine aren't. I mean, no . . . I love them, my parents, they're
so so great—they paid for my apartment here and they're super
supportive about my work, so I'm not badmouthing them, at all—
but they are totally just regular people as far as looks go . . .
very normal./ Average.

PAIGE Exactly./ Mine too . . . I mean . . . no, that's not fair, because
my mom was kinda hot when she was young, nice body, I think,
and . . . anyhow . . . she was a *catch* back in her day, but my
dad's, like . . . you know, just a guy. Very ordinary. Not what I'd

call handsome—nice hair, he always had nice hair—but *some*thing about the two of them together and BAM! Here I am . . .

KATE Same for me. *Now*. I mean, I grew into my looks is all I'm saying . . . I was awkward in my teens, that's what I mean . . .

PAIGE Yeah, but now you're *very* pretty . . . like, in an *unusual* way . . . but yeah . . . pretty.

KATE Thanks . . . that's really . . . you too.

PAIGE And that's what I *mean* . . . here we are . . . just trying to make it in a really tough business and on top of that, we've gotta deal with the fact that we're these two extremely attractive women.

KATE No, I know what you're saying . . . it can be a *real* drawback sometimes . . .

PAIGE Definitely! It *definitely* can . . . even more than being an asset. More often than not.

KATE Yeah . . . I mean . . . at least sometimes.

PAIGE Often.

KAYE You think?

PAIGE A *lot* of the time. Yes.

KATE I do get sick of being stared at. (*Beat.*) Know what I mean? Like on the subway, or just . . . / Or *elevators* . . . ?

PAIGE Oh fuck yes!/ God! I HATE that!

KATE It's, like . . . gimme a break, ok? I'm just trying to get home . . . I'm trapped in here with you, so just . . . time out! (*Making a hand gesture for effect.*) / TIME OUT, GUYS!

PAIGE *nods vigorously at this and stomps one foot. Claps.*

PAIGE Shit yeah!/ HATE-THAT. Hate it.

KATE I mean . . . like you said: it's not some big invitation to people—men *or* women—just because you have long legs or a nice ass or this killer body . . . a face like yours. Or mine, I guess.

(*Beat.*) I mean . . . God! Stop staring already!! Does that even make sense? What I'm saying?

PAIGE I mean . . . like you're reading off a page in my *diary*! I'm serious! I *so* feel that same way! (*Beat.*) I'm not responsible for this. It's just *me*. (*Points.*) I'm not working to draw attention to myself . . . I am totally natural. Every *inch* of me . . . so just . . . I mean . . . whatever . . . just back off! Right?

KATE *looks over at* PAIGE. *Gives her the once over. Nods at her breasts. Points.*

KATE Yeah! Wait . . . (*Points.*) . . . even . . . *those*?

PAIGE Completely. Natural.

KATE *is frankly surprised by this fact. Takes a beat.*

KATE Wow. *God.* Good for you.

PAIGE *Hardly.* (*Beat.*) Trust me . . .

KATE I wouldn't know.

KATE *turns to* PAIGE, *showing off her lovely but much less curvy figure.*

PAIGE Yeah? Well, then, you're lucky.

KATE Why's that?

PAIGE You just . . . believe me, you *are*. The shit I've gone through because of . . . whatever. Biology. Anatomy. Genetics. *Something.* (*Beat.*) Fucking sucks.

KATE I guess.

PAIGE I mean . . . don't get me wrong . . . they get me through the door./ Depending on the *door*, of course . . .

KATE Ha! I'll bet./ All the way to the *couch*, probably...

PAIGE No, come on! Seriously . . . sometimes they do help . . . a little . . . *but* . . .

KATE . . . what . . . ?

PAIGE Mostly they suck.

KATE Yeah?

PAIGE Yep. Suck hard. Like *cancer.*/ Not like terminal cancer but one of the other kinds./ The type you recover from. One of those kinds of cancer. The *good* kind.

KATE Excuse me?/ Come *on.*/ There's no *good* . . . you shouldn't say things like that. It's not . . . that's unlucky. To do that.

PAIGE Yeah, no, that's true. Maybe not *cancer*. But, like . . . something bad. (*Beat.*) Polio.

KATE Ha! (*Laughs.*) Really? A *disease*?

PAIGE Sometimes! (*Beat.*) I'm not kidding . . . plus my *back*, and the *bras* with all the . . . they suck.

KATE Ok. (*Beat.*) That just seems . . .

PAIGE Look, I'm sure you get it in *other* ways, you're totally attractive . . . look at you!

KATE . . . thanks, but . . .

PAIGE So you know what I'm saying! Guys staring at you . . . other girls hating you . . . never being taken seriously! It fucking *sucks*.

KATE No . . . *that* does makes total sense.

PAIGE Plus everybody thinks they're *fake*, anyway . . . so that *really* sucks! I mean, come on! "*Fake*?!"

KATE Yeah. No. I get it./ That's . . .

PAIGE Thanks./ Anyway, good luck.

KATE Yep. You too.

PAIGE *nods and smiles. Stands up with her pages, paces as she works on them.* KATE *watches her, then asks:*

You're here for "the daughter," right? "Susan?" I mean, obviously . . .

PAIGE 'Course.

KATE Ok. Cool./ I figured . . .

PAIGE Yeah./ It's the best part, so . . .

KATE I agree. Lovely. It's just . . . *flawless*, I think. An amazing part for someone our . . . you know. Age. Type. (*Beat.*) I usually go in for such . . . *crap*. It's just so nice to finally read something that you *want*. I'm just, like, *desperate* for this!/ LOVE it!

PAIGE Yeah, me too./ Killer part./ Edgy.

KATE Right./ Yes . . . but edgy in a . . . kind of a tender way . . . edgy but tender . . . I mean . . . that "death" scene . . .?/ That thing is just . . . crazy good!/ CRAZY. GOOD.

PAIGE I know!/ I *love* that scene!/ *SO* good!!

KATE I was doing it this morning—I like to rehearse in the park— so I was doing it, just going through the lines, I mean . . . I've got the *pages*, in my hand, but I'm on this bench and I'm . . . you know . . . with the cough and, like, the . . . she's crying but being brave— I think she's *so* brave, this character, don't you? Like *seriously* brave—and I'm doing that . . . coughing and weeping and, and . . . people gather. Around me. A lot of *tourists*, I think, but folks from here, too, and I'm just *rehearsing*! Running lines! But I do the whole coughing thing plus I start crying . . . and once I'm going it's, like, uncontrollable . . . And people are standing there . . . open-mouthed, or they're, whatever, snapping photos on their phones. A crowd gathers. I'm not kidding you. A *crowd* . . . (*Beat.*) And I'm just thinking to myself—I, like, step outside myself as this is happening, I'm watching me *and* the people *and* this Asian guy getting the whole thing on his iPad—I step out of it as it's happening and I think . . . *wow* . . . this scene is going to be incredible! I mean, once it's rehearsed and on set and you've got a director there, *challenging* you and *willing* you to go further with your fellow actors, this thing is gonna be just . . . I don't even have words for it . . . you know? That's what this is gonna be like . . . something

they don't even have *words* for yet. The guy at *The Times* will
have to make up words for it . . . it's *that* good . . . (*Beat.*) Anyway,
I checked YouTube earlier but I haven't seen it up there yet . . .
(*She explains.*) The footage that the Asian guy took . . .

PAIGE *nods at this, taking in the magnitude of what* KATE *is describing.*

PAIGE Huh.

KATE Yeah.

PAIGE Wow. That's . . . I usually run lines with my boyfriend and he
can barely speak.

KATE Oh, right! You date that football guy./ On the Jets.

PAIGE Yeah./ Uh-huh, but he never says nice things about my work,
I mean . . . (*Beat.*) Fuck that. I'm gonna try running lines in the park
next time. That sounds great.

KATE It is. It totally works . . .

PAIGE I guess! (*Beat.*) Anyway, I'll give you my email. Let me know if
that thing shows up on-line 'cause I'd love to see it . . .

KATE Okay. I will. For sure. I might add it to my reel . . . (*Beat.*) I think
we should definitely exchange info, stay in touch. Us *sistas* gotta
stick together. Right?!/ (*Smiles.*) That'd be awesome.

PAIGE Absolutely./ (*Smiles.*) Anyway . . . good luck!

KATE Thanks! You too.

*They smile at each other but then look away—not sure if they're
telling the truth about how "great" it would be.*

I mean . . . I *feel* like we've been in a lot of the same classes and
stuff or, maybe like . . . ? *Years* ago?

PAIGE . . . or a workshop . . . maybe? Over at MTC or one of those?
The Public? (*Both girls nod at this.*) Yeah . . . seems like it to me,
too. Totally.

KATE . . . *any-way* . . .

PAIGE Yeah. (*Beat.*) We should stay in touch or whatever . . . I'm sorry, what's your name again? I'm *terrible* with names!

KATE It's "Kate." With a "T."

PAIGE Right! "Kate." Nice.

KATE Anyway . . . good luck!

PAIGE You too!

They turn back to what they're doing. PAIGE *looking over her lines and* KATE *going through her beauty routine.*

KATE *pulls out a teasing comb and looks around. Starts wildly pulling at her hair with the instrument.*

KATE (*Explaining.*) . . . just wanna . . . you know . . .

PAIGE I get it! Add a little volume? (*Points.*) I just threw mine up in a bun—I thought it said the character had her hair up in a bun—but that looks great./ Very chic.

KATE Thanks!/ I've been running around all day.

PAIGE Nice. Auditions?

KATE Ummmm . . . yes. That and, you know . . . other stuff./ Class and over to Equity . . . *stuff.*

PAIGE Right./ 'Course.

KATE Just "acting" stuff.

PAIGE Me too.

KATE Yeah?

PAIGE Yep. "Pilot Season," so . . . you know . . . ABC has me under contract but I'm still free to get out there and— (*Beat.*) Whatever! This whole business is crazy!!

KATE *shakes her head firmly in agreement at this statement. Apparently she and* PAIGE *are simpatico on this.*

KATE God yes! It's *nuts.*

PAIGE No shit! Like . . . *certifiably* nuts . . .

KATE *Right?* All these opportunities . . . I feel like *this* is *really* gonna be my year . . . this year or next year.

PAIGE . . . that's so cool . . . good luck!

KATE Thanks! You too.

PAIGE That'd be great if one of us gets this. "The daughter." Such a break-out part.

KATE Absolutely.

PAIGE My agent says CBS is thinking about her as a potential series regular . . .

KATE *No!* Really?/ I love the death scene . . . I hope they don't cut that.

PAIGE Yep./ It's a guest spot now but they're considering her for a six episode arc and maybe a full-on regular if they're picked up again next year.

KATE WOW./ That's . . .

PAIGE I *know,* right?/ It's *exactly* what I need right now . . .

KATE Sweet.

PAIGE Uh-huh. (*Beat.*) Anyway . . . good luck.

KATE Thanks. You too. (*Beat.*) Definitely.

KATE *smiles and goes back to doing her hair.* PAIGE *looks down at the pages again. Finally,* KATE *speaks to her:*

I'm actually between agencies . . .

PAIGE Oh. Too bad. Shit.

KATE Yeah.

PAIGE That's hard.

KATE I know. (*Beat.*) I've got this *manager,* but . . .

PAIGE A good manager is great.

KATE No, that's true . . . of *course* . . .

PAIGE Makes a *huge* difference.

KATE Yep. But . . . an *agent* . . .

PAIGE Well . . . I mean . . . you *gotta* have an agent in this business . . . if you wanna survive!

KATE True.

PAIGE No, but I mean you *have* to have one./ No question.

KATE I know./ Right, but . . .

PAIGE HAVE-TO. Imperative.

KATE Okay . . . I *know*. Sure.

PAIGE Because if you don't . . . like, if you don't have one . . . or are in-between or whatever you are . . . or got, say, *dropped* even . . .

KATE I didn't!! It's a *transitional* thing . . . I'm just playing the field a bit, seeing who's the best fit for me and who'll be my best *advocate* and . . . they didn't drop me. At all./ They did *not*.

PAIGE No, God!/ I'm not saying that about *you*! I'm just saying a person, if you're some *person* who had that happen . . . if you *were* to be kicked out by your agency . . . let go or happened to be released as a client . . .

KATE I really wasn't! I don't want you to be thinking that, because . . . it's not true!

PAIGE . . . I'm just saying *hypothetically* . . .

KATE Yeah, but it makes me feel bad, because *mine* left . . . my agent left—she had this *skin* thing—and she was really great and hard-working for her clients . . . which I *loved* . . . but . . .

PAIGE My people are shit. I mean, they're *huge*, CAA, they're massive and they're amazing but sometimes they're shit, too, do you know what I mean by that? (*Beat.*) Amazing while simultaneously managing to be this *steaming* pile of shit . . . at the same time?

KATE . . . I *think* so . . .

PAIGE It's just . . . it's *so* competitive, just at the agency!! All the

Emmas and *Jessicas* and *Jennifers* and everybody . . . and all
of us out there vying for the *same* thing, the *same* little . . . bits
of bread . . .

KATE . . . the crumbs . . .

PAIGE *Yes*! And sometimes not even that! They're not even crumbs
. . . *bits* of crumbs! A tiny piece of a bit of a crumb!

KATE *Crumbs* of crumbs . . .

PAIGE Exactly! YES! God, I've never heard it put that way but yes!
Exactly like that! "Crumbs of crumbs." (*Beat.*) You're, like, an "old
soul" or something, aren't you?

KATE I mean . . . *kind* of . . .

PAIGE I can tell! No, seriously, I can . . .

KATE *nods at this, realizing just how similar they are. A smile between
them.*

Anyway. Good luck.

KATE Yeah. You too. (*Beat.*) You too . . .

They smile and nod again. KATE *looks off toward a door. Checks the
time on her phone. Looks back over at* PAIGE.

PAIGE Knock on wood! Right?

KATE Exactly! (*Beat.*) Or "Touch wood."

PAIGE Hmmmm?

KATE "Touch wood." It's the same thing. It's what they say in London
for "Good luck." "Touch wood." (*Beat.*) I studied at *RADA*.

PAIGE Nice! I love London. Love to work there.

KATE Me too. Can't wait to. (*Beat.*) Anyway . . . Break a leg.

PAIGE Right, yes, right! You as well . . .

KATE Thanks.

PAIGE I mean with everything . . .

KATE *doesn't exactly understand what* PAIGE *means by this.*

KATE Excuse me?

PAIGE Not just this . . . "the daughter" . . . I mean with *everything.*
Getting another agent. That sort of thing. All of it./ The whole
"career" part of your . . . life . . .

KATE Ahhhh. I see./ Well . . . thanks.

PAIGE You bet.

KATE Will do.

PAIGE Get the agent *first* . . . trust me. (*Smiles.*) You gotta have an
agent!

KATE I know you do! That's just . . . yes. There's no way around that.
I *know* . . .

PAIGE Not that I'm aware of, no. Ya gotta have one!

KATE Okay, good, I get it! Got it! I *need* an agent! O-kay!! Thank
you!! I GET IT!!!!

A moment of tension. KATE *starts to go back to her own preparation
when* PAIGE *calls out to her. Making peace:*

PAIGE Hey . . . would you wanna run lines?/ Sorry. Wanna run lines?

KATE Hmmm?/ Ahhhh . . .

PAIGE Just—only if it helps you—I got this late last night and I didn't
quite get the whole thing down yet . . . so . . . I just thought . . .

KATE *thinks about this. Considering.*

KATE Oh. Ummmm . . . (*Looking at* PAIGE.) Ok. Sure. Let's run 'em.

KATE *turns and gets out her sides. Scans the lines.*

So . . . (*Reading.*) . . . should we start with the . . . how did you
deal with the *Farsi*?

PAIGE Excuse me?

KATE The "Farsi." The Persian language in the second side . . . how did you handle that?

PAIGE Oh God! You mean all the . . . ?! (*Scribbles in mid-air.*) I *dunno*! I was just gonna . . .

KATE Wait, *what's* . . . ? (*She mimes the scribbles.*)

PAIGE Just . . . the way those people write words.

KATE I think it actually goes in the opposite direction. (*Mimes this.*) Right to left . . .

PAIGE Oh. Huh. Anyway, I figured I could *fake* my way through that part at the audition, and then when I get cast—I mean *if*, if I get cast—then I'd get help from a tutor or something . . . a linguist that the network would hire . . . or whatever. That's probably how they do it . . . (*Beat.*) Right? I'm just saying, like, when I played a prostitute on *Homeland* or on that, umm, one show . . . *24* . . . that's how they did it there. With a specialist.

KATE Oh. So . . . you played a . . . prostitute on *both* of those shows? Really?

PAIGE Yeah. Not the *same* one. Different ones. One was a red-head. (*Beat.*) Anyway, I'm thinking I could kinda just fake my way through it. Like make that sound they do when somebody dies or that type of thing. (*Makes noise like a Middle Eastern woman in mourning.*) I'm saying just for *now* . . .

KATE Yeah. No, I'm sure you can do it that way if you *need* to./ That'll be *fine*. If you can't do it the other way . . .

PAIGE Cool./ Wait . . . what do you mean? Did you actually learn those parts? I mean . . . *in Farsi*?

KATE Yeah.

PAIGE You *did*?! (*Beat.*) Wow. (*Beat.*) *Shit*.

KATE I just think it helps . . .

PAIGE I mean . . . *yeah*! That's *incredible*!

KATE Hopefully they'll appreciate it in the room. You never know, but hey, fingers crossed. (*Smiling.*) "Touch wood."

PAIGE That's amazing.

KATE You do what you gotta do. I'm sure you'll be great in the other section, that first bit. Where she . . . takes her shirt off.

PAIGE *Terrific.*

KATE No! I mean . . . I'm sure that's not the only reason they've called you in . . . just for that./ Probably not . . .

PAIGE Maybe!/ God, it sure feels like it *now* . . .

KATE No, I'm *sure* it's more than that. I mean, you're so good . . . and you had a series . . . / That cancelled series . . .

PAIGE True./ Wow . . . so, if you don't mind . . . you know, letting me pick your brain for a second . . .

KATE No, no, no. Pick away.

PAIGE I just . . . how did you do it? So quickly, I mean . . . all the . . .?

KATE What? The *language* stuff?

PAIGE *nods her head and slides down another chair or two.*

PAIGE Yeah! They sent it over *really* late last night . . . I didn't even have time to read the whole script and . . . you managed to . . .!

KATE You got the whole script?

PAIGE Of *course*. I'm at CAA. We always get the whole script . . ./ Some guy from CAA *wrote* the script!

KATE Wow. That's . . . / It's nice to be "wanted."

PAIGE That's true, it's usually great, but . . . like I said before . . . so *what*? Here I am, ready to go in there with producers and network execs and I'm not even prepared! FUCK! This really . . . just . . . !

KATE Sucks?

PAIGE Yes! IT SUCKS! *Damn* it . . . I'm gonna just *go off* on somebody later! At least somebody's *assistant*!

KATE I *know* . . . I hate it when they throw you a curveball like that . . .

PAIGE This isn't even . . . it's like murder! It's *like* they're actually
murdering me!/ Sending me in there to be murdered!!

KATE *No.*/ Not quite. It's bad, don't get me wrong—looking *foolish* is
bad—but it's not . . . murder. (*Beat.*) True?

PAIGE Ok, no, maybe not that. Not murder. But incest. It's like that
. . . (*Beat.*) I mean, these guys are *supposed* to be my family!
Right?! They are my "family" and they're *fucking* me over so
that's . . . what else're you gonna call it if not that?! Right?! It's
incest.

KATE *nods her head, trying to be sympathetic.* PAIGE *is just not happy
about this.*

KATE I get it. Maybe not the "incest" part . . . I've only got sisters . . .
but I know that feeling in my gut . . . when I've gone into auditions
and *really* blown it./ And not even just blown it but, like, *so* totally
and completely embarrassed myself that I've felt like leaving the
industry or, like, I should be in some other line of work because of
my *total* lack of preparation. Yeah. I *definitely* know that feeling . . .

PAIGE *is nodding her head while* KATE *is talking. She is feeling this—
suddenly very nervous about her audition.*

PAIGE Shit./ Fuck!/ (*Beat.*) Fuck, fuck, fuck!!/ FUCK!!!

KATE . . . it's okay./ You're gonna be fine . . . / Probably.

PAIGE I don't even know where to begin with some of this shit!!

KATE It's a tricky language. It's beautiful when you hear it, but it's
tricky . . .

PAIGE Shit!! I was just gonna make that funny noise and read the English translation that they've got here . . .

KATE Good. *Cool* . . . I'm sure that's what most people are doing . . .

PAIGE Yeah, but not *you*! You went and learned the damn thing . . . !!

KATE No, that's not . . . I just brushed up on it. With Rosetta Stone . . .

PAIGE *Really*? That crap they sell at the *mall*?

KATE Yeah. (*Whispering.*) I mean . . . I feel like I'm cheating a bit, because . . . my mother's Persian./ Well, half. She's half Persian.

PAIGE She *is*?/ *Really*?!

KATE Absolutely. From Iran. Well, her *mom* was.

PAIGE FUCK! That's *so* lucky! My mom's from fucking *Tucson*!! That sucks!!! I always hated Arizona and now I hate it even more!!

KATE Yep. So I've been speaking Farsi . . . a few words and phrases, anyway . . . for most of my life.

PAIGE *So* cool! That's . . . (*Studying her.*) God, you do *not* look Middle Eastern. You're *so* pretty . . .

KATE Well, like I said . . . it's just half. *Half* of a half, actually . . . which is . . . God, I hate *math*! (*Thinks.*) Lemme see.

They both think about this for a minute—unsure what the answer to the equation would be. Even counting it out on their fingers.

PAIGE Anyway . . . you're "part," right? You're at least "'part" Middle Eastern. (*Beat.*) Which I can kinda see now . . . like I said, in the eyes. You have *such* exotic eyes!

KATE Thank you.

PAIGE You'd look really good in the . . . (*Miming.*) . . . you know . . . with the thing covering up your head . . . and the . . .

KATE A "burka?"'

PAIGE Yes! One of those! You'd look amazing in one . . . that *eye-hole* thingie would really flatter you . . .

KATE Thanks, I guess. (*Beat.*) Just so you know, though . . . I'm a
Lutheran . . .

PAIGE No! I wasn't being rude . . . no offense! I honestly meant it as
a *compliment* . . .

KATE . . . thanks . . .

PAIGE *realizes that* KATE *doesn't like this so much so she tries connecting by explaining herself:*

PAIGE I really did! (*Beat.*) Some people—some *actors*—would not
take it like that, but I really did mean it that way. I think you're
totally nice looking.

KATE That's sweet. Thank you.

PAIGE You're *really* "Middle Eastern?" God, you don't have any of
the . . . *sideburns* or . . .

KATE Well, like I said. It is just half.

PAIGE *Half* of half.

KATE Right . . . which is . . . like . . . (*Thinking.*) Ahhh! Fractions!
Whatever! Anyway, not that much!! Plus my dad is *Norwegian* . . .

PAIGE Oh! Well, *that* explains it . . . I love all those countries up there
. . . Sweden, and . . . (*Thinks.*) Iceland! *Such* beautiful people!

KATE *half-smiles and starts to speak when* BREE *returns. She looks around the room. Checks her clipboard, then exits.*

KATE *stands, taking a step toward her. She turns and speaks to* PAIGE*:*

KATE God, they're taking *forever* with that girl who's in there now
. . . it's kind of starting to freak me out . . .

PAIGE Fuck, I wonder if they just *gave* her the part or something?!!
Probably!!/ Shit!!! That bitch . . . they probably *love* her for this,
and it's *such* a good part! I HAVE *GOTTA* READ FOR THIS PART!!

FUCK!! I HAVE TO!! *HAVE*-TO!! I'M SERIOUSLY NOT GOING
HOME WITHOUT READING FOR THIS PART!! I WON'T! NO! NO,
NO, NO, NO, NO, NO, NO!!

KATE Yeah, *probably*!/ You okay there . . . ?

PAIGE *is getting herself worked up. She takes a breath.*

PAIGE I'm not *ranting*, I'm really not, just blowing off some steam
but . . . you know . . . nobody over at CAA told me to go learn
Farsi!! Nobody on my team told me I might as well play the lottery
every day and hope to win a Mega *Billion* and *buy* my *own* fucking
broadcast network, the likelihood of me ever being cast on a
good show . . . *especially* being an actor who's based in fucking
New York!!

KATE I hear you. I feel that all the time . . .

PAIGE Yeah, but at *least* you speak *Persian*!!

KATE It's just so much of the moment, I think. So much pain and
suffering going on there in the Middle East and TV's very quick to
pick up on that . . .

PAIGE That's true. Most of my favorite shows do some kind of terror-
ist component. (*Beat.*) Shit! That's *so* dumb of me not to connect
the dots! FUCK!!

PAIGE *knocks her bag to the floor. Clearly frustrated.*

KATE Anyway . . . there's still time . . .

PAIGE For what?

KATE I guess I can . . . I mean, I can steer you through the basics
. . . just so you don't sound like a complete *idiot* in there . . .

Silence. The wheels begin to slowly turn in KATE'*s head.*

PAIGE That's . . . you'd *do* that?! For *me*? Another actor . . . I mean . . . an actor that you're in *direct* competition with?

KATE Sure. We're all in this together . . . right?

PAIGE Yeah! Absolutely . . . I mean, I can't help that I'm a bit further ahead but yeah . . . we're all in the same boat. Essentially. (*Beat.*) Just the first lines, help me with the first couple and then I can just . . . you know . . . I'll start crying or something, get their minds off it through my tears. (*Beat.*) I'm an *amazing* fake cryer.

KATE I'll *bet.* (*Beat.*) Ok, fine, so, let's . . .

PAIGE *grabs her stuff and slides down a couple of seats.*

PAIGE Alright . . . so this first part—and some of this is just backstory —but here where Susan's begging for her husband's life . . .

KATE . . . right . . .

PAIGE . . . but in a kind of comical way . . .

KATE Uh-huh.

PAIGE Like she's crying, but she's still a funny person . . . she's still *amusing* . . .

KATE . . . and sexy . . .

PAIGE Right . . . and sexy . . . and she wanders over to that "guard," the one with that big gun in his hands, and she's, like . . . it takes a second for her to realize that she's made it this far . . . into the *lair* of her enemy—without weapons, without back-up—simply because she is who she is: a beautiful woman, with brains and guts and, and . . . and . . .

KATE Nice breasts. (*Beat.*) It says that in my pages. "Nice breasts." Does it in yours?

PAIGE Yeah, it does. Yes.

KATE I mean, mine are nice—I've always felt that they were, anyway, but—yours are probably more what they're looking for.

PAIGE We'll see . . . whatever. That's not, like, her *main* focus in this
scene . . . anyhow, Susan's there. Right there. *Inches* away from
being reunited with her husband . . . David . . . *but* there's this
guard there. Achmed. He's the son of her friends—Bashir and
Pasha—and he's standing in front of her. She's gotta get past him.
So she opens her mouth, licks her lips . . . (*Mimes this.*) And then
she speaks. Speaks to Achmed—this is in the script not on the
sides, so you probably weren't even aware of their . . . oh shit!
This is where she has her hair up in a bun! *That's* why you didn't
know about the . . . anyway—she and this guy, the one guard
guy? Achmed? They're *actually* lovers . . .

KATE *No!/ Really?*

PAIGE YES./ That's what it says . . . unless they plan on re-writing it . . .

KATE *thinks about this for a moment. Truly surprised by this new piece
of information that she didn't have.*

KATE Susan and *that* guy are lovers? The *guard?* "Achmed?"

PAIGE Yep. I think so. That's what it says.

KATE Shit! That's—by the way, you're actually pretty good with
names. (*Beat.*) But geez, thanks! That *totally* changes the way
I was approaching this thing. *Huh.* Wow . . . (*To* PAIGE.) I appreciate it.

PAIGE No problem. *Sista.* (*A thin smile.*) So . . . would you actually
do that . . . right now? Help me understand a little bit of this, even
just the first line or two? (*Beat.*) That'd be SO great . . .

KATE Sure. Of *course.* Let's see . . . (*Pointing.*) I'll just write it out here
in the margin so that you can . . . do you have a pen?

PAIGE *looks around, scoops up her bag and digs in it. Finally produces
a pen. Hands it over.*

PAIGE This is so nice of you! I'm gonna give you my agent's details
after this . . . I really am./ I mean, like, his assistant.

KATE Thanks./ Thank you.

PAIGE Of course!

KATE It'll only take a minute. (*Writing.*) Just lemme think . . . I'll write it out in a way that you can understand it. Phonetically. (*Serious.*) And promise me, when speaking the language, to use your entire mouth. Tongue, teeth, lips. The *key* to Farsi is spit.

KATE *demonstrates and* PAIGE *tries to copy her movements.* KATE *looks on approvingly. Pats her on the back.*

KATE *turns to* PAIGE*'s script and starts writing as* PAIGE *looks around, decides to go for it. Jumps up.*

PAIGE Hey . . . do you mind if I go to the bathroom while you're doing that? I'll only be a few seconds but my *bladder* . . . it's always a killer right before I go in the room! (*Indicates.*) Plus, I just wanna get . . .

KATE No problem. I know the drill!! I've gone *twice* already!/ (*Smiles.*) If they call you I'll let 'em know you'll be right back.

PAIGE Great!/ That's *so* great! And I will give you that number after, okay?/ On our way out.

KATE Sure./ *Perfect.*

PAIGE Thanks. (*Beat.*) And hey, listen . . . if they bring *you* in first, before I get back . . . then . . . you know . . .

KATE *What?*

PAIGE Nothing. I just wanted to say: good luck!

KATE Thanks! You too!

PAIGE Hey . . . how do you say *that* in Farsi? "Good luck?" How does that sound?

KATE *Oh. Ummmm . . . (In Farsi.) Pren-tu-mesh.*

PAIGE Ha! Cool. Okay. Well . . . "pren-tu-mesh!"

KATE Yeah. You too. Pren-tu-mesh Kell-*shez*! (*Beat.*) That means "Best of luck to you!"

PAIGE *smiles and hurries off, headed to the ladies' room. She turns and looks back at* KATE. *Takes a step toward her as she says:*

PAIGE Ahhhh . . . you're not just writing gibberish there . . . are you? To make me look stupid?/ No, I just . . . mean . . . *some* people might . . .

KATE Come *on.*/ Would I do that? To a *sista*?

PAIGE *thinks about it. Nods. Smiles, turns and walks off—she looks back one time as she exits:*

PAIGE "Pren-tu-mesh!"

KATE *waves as* PAIGE *leaves. A moment or two passes and the* BREE *walks into the room. Looks around.*

BREE Paige? Is there a "Paige" here? (*Looking at* KATE.) Are you "Paige Parsons?"

KATE No. You mean that "blonde girl?" The one who was right over there?

BREE I don't know. *Guess* so. You guys all look the same to me. (*Looks again at her list.*) Someone named *Paige Parsons.* That's all the info I've got here.

KATE Yeah . . . that's her. (*Beat.*) I think she *left.* She took her stuff and just . . . / Yep. An *emergency* or some . . . kinda . . .

BREE Really?/ Oh . . . ok. Whatever. Thanks.

KATE Sure. Happy to help.

BREE I guess you're next. You might as well come in now . . . (*Reading.*) Are you "Kate?"

KATE Yeah . . . "Kate Carlson." Great. So lemme just . . . I'll be there in one minute.

BREE *nods at* KATE. *Looks around one more time, then checks* PAIGE *off her list and disappears.*

KATE *smiles to herself, finishes writing out another line of dialogue on* PAIGE*'s sides. She sets them down on the chair. She thinks about it, grabs them again and writes:*

(*To herself.*) "Pren-tu-mesh." (*Beat.*) Bitch . . .

She finishes. Calmly places the sides and the pen on the chair. She packs her things and heads into the audition. Looking tall and beautiful and confident.

One last look around the room. She smiles and starts to exit.

Suddenly KATE *stops, remembering something she needs to do. She digs in her purse and pulls out a pair of silicone breast enhancers ("chicken cutlets") in a Ziploc baggie. Looks around and quickly slips them inside her bra. Adjusts them and checks herself out. Satisfied with the result,* KATE *marches off toward her audition.*

A moment passes. PAIGE *enters and sits back down. Looks around. No* KATE. *Picks up her sides and reads:*

PAIGE "Pren-tu-mesh." Ahhh, that's sweet . . . (*Beat.*) Okay, come on, come on . . . let's do this.

She looks over toward the door as she shakes her head. Finally goes back to her sides.

PAIGE *tries to quietly work on the Farsi dialogue.*

"... and now it's come to this, has it? The end of the road for you and me ..." (*She now tries this in phonetic Farsi.*) "Fac-a-lac-a-lac-a-shed-maka-het-mala." Fuck. That's *hard*. (*Tries it one more time.*) "Fac-a-lac-a-lac-a-shed-maka-het-mala." That *can't* be right! Can it ...? Fac-a-lac-a-lac-a-shed-maka-het-mala. SHIT! Ok, Again. "Fac-a-lac-a-lac-a-shed-maka-het-mala ..." Damn it. One more time. "Fac-a-lac-a-lac-a-shed-maka-het-mala."

PAIGE *sits alone, waiting for her chance to audition for the wonderful role of "the daughter." She continues to work on saying the words in her badly broken version of Farsi.*

Silence. Darkness.

squeeze play

Squeeze Play had its world premiere at the Mile High Theatre, Hoboken, NJ, in June 2013 as part of a benefit called "7th Inning Stretch" (in a version that featured a "Mom" instead of a "Dad"). It was directed by Chris O'Connor.

COACH Victor Slezak
MOM   Barbara Pitts

Silence. Darkness.

Two men standing on a baseball field. Local park sort of backstop, not a professional situation.

*One man (*THE DAD*) wearing Brooks Brothers casual. Another man (*THE COACH*) is decked out in training gear. Carrying a clip board with forms.*

DAD   . . . beautiful day.

COACH   Uh-huh. It sure is.

The men stand quietly for a moment. Each staring off in different directions.

In fact, they should never look at each other throughout.

DAD   . . . I know what you're thinking.

COACH   Yeah? (*Beat.*) What's that?

DAD   No, I don't mean *exactly*—like, I'm a mind reader or something —I just mean in general. I know "in general" what you're thinking right now. How you're feeling.

COACH   Is that so?

DAD   Probably.

COACH   And?

DAD   You're disgusted. Right?

COACH Pretty much. Yep.

DAD I can tell.

COACH . . .

DAD Well . . . that's . . . what would you do?

COACH *Me*?

DAD Yes. I'm just saying . . . in my situation?

COACH I dunno.

DAD Yes you do. (*Beat.*) I'm not being rude . . . I'm just saying that I can tell you think I'm an asshole for asking you this so you must have an idea of what the *right* thing to do would be. (*Beat.*) True?

COACH I guess I do. Yeah.

DAD Which is . . . ?

COACH You *know*.

DAD Yeah, I probably do . . . I have an idea what you're going to say . . . what most people in this situation would say . . . like, what MY dad would've said if he was you . . . (*Beat.*) I'm just curious about what *you're* going to say.

The two men stand looking into the distance. Watching the boys practice across the great expanse of lawn in front of them.

COACH I'm gonna say I wish you'd never asked me this. I wanna say "fuck you" and spit in your face and tell you that's not how we play this game and throw your kid off the team and make an example of him. And you. That's what I *wanna* do. And say. I would like to do that . . . right now. This minute.

DAD I see.

COACH That's what I'd *expect* to happen if I was a parent whose kid was on my team, if you did this and I heard about it . . . I'd come to me and complain and point fingers and do everything I could—go down to see one of those people at the "Y" or over at the City Hall . . . *somewhere*—and complain about you and your conduct . . . *that's* the kind of thing I'd expect of myself or other folks I know. If I found out about it.

DAD Okay. Fair enough. (*Beat.*) But that's not what you're going to do. Right? Is it?

COACH No. I don't suppose I am . . .

DAD And why is that?

COACH You know why.

DAD I guess I do.

COACH Yeah, I guess you do. In fact, I'm *sure* you do. (*Beat.*) I figure that's why you even had the balls to ask me this . . . to have the *guts* to ask another man to do something like you're asking me here.

DAD Maybe so.

COACH Because you knew I'd have to think about it. I'd have to give it some very *serious* consideration, thanks to the place I find myself in currently. The state of my life at the present time. (*Beat.*) *So.*

DAD It's a tough economy.

COACH Yeah, it certainly is.

DAD Hard to keep a job. Or find one again . . .

COACH Exactly.

DAD And money is tight. For families who are *struggling* . . . bills to pay . . .

COACH Yep.

DAD A kid in college.

COACH Exactly.

DAD I get that.

COACH *Yeah?* You do?

DAD I absolutely do . . . it's very hard these days. To make ends meet.

COACH But you're willing to help me with that.

DAD I am. Yes.

COACH You're . . . *what* . . . ? Tell me again?

DAD I'm happy to . . . you know . . .

COACH No, I don't. I don't know exactly because of the way you
said it. Just sorta tossed it up in the air . . . like a screwball or a,
you know, some kind of *curve* that you've thrown at me . . . just
floating there over the plate. Waiting for me to take a swing at it.

DAD That's very *poetic*.

COACH Fuck. You.

DAD I'm not trying to be funny. I just like the way you put it . . .
that analogy. It's true. I did kind of just *drop* it there. Like that.
In your lap.

COACH Yeah, well—I guess you do what you gotta do.

DAD That's right. (*Beat.*) You do.

COACH Whatever.

THE DAD *turns and looks at* THE COACH. *Watching him.* THE COACH
doesn't turn to meet his gaze.

DAD And I do feel that . . . not that I have to but I *need* to. *Want* to,
even. I *want* to give my kid a chance . . . something I don't think
I ever really got when I was his age . . . and my dad was even
our coach! Of my little league team, isn't that crazy? He was the
coach and he made me just sit there, watch the other guys play
because they were better. (*Beat.*) He wanted to win more than
he wanted me to play and learn and have fun. Dad wanted to
win *trophies* and beat the other dads who weren't using *their*
sons on *their* teams . . . that's how I grew up and I don't want
that for my kid. I want him to play now . . . this year. On a great
team, even if he's not good enough or the best or anything like

that. *That* is what I'm willing to pay you to do. Is to make him feel like he's got a chance.

COACH I get it.

DAD Thanks.

COACH Doesn't mean I like it. Or like you for doing it . . .

DAD I understand.

COACH . . . but I get *why* you're doing it. It's a fucked up way of seeing things, but I do follow your line of thinking.

DAD I'm glad.

COACH It's just . . . he's never gonna make it. You know that, right?

DAD What do you mean?

COACH Your kid. (*Beat.*) I can tell, even at this age. Some guys, they grow into the game—not even that, "grow" into it but it's a thing where they just get better and they get bigger and faster and stronger and it just occurs. Suddenly you've got a really good little ballplayer on your hands. Or it happens in school, middle school or even in high school occasionally, it just happens and one of these boys'll become a major talent almost overnight, just outta nowhere. But not your son. No way. (*Beat.*) You're giving 'em hope that doesn't exist. We can do this . . . I can put him out there and I can listen to the other players and the moms and dads yelling at me, telling me I'm crazy for playing him, even out in right field they'll think I'm some sorta fucking nutjob for doing it . . . but this is it . . . right here. I don't even think he'll get on a team next year, the skills he's got. I just want you to know the truth . . .

DAD No, I know. I know it. (*Beat.*) Yes.

COACH You're just delaying this. The fact that this game's not for him.

DAD I get that. I do.

COACH Okay. Just so you do.

DAD I just . . . I wanna give him this *moment*. A few games where he's out there with his friends and . . . you know . . . gets to run out on the field with those guys, not just be on the bench, sitting there, watching . . . waiting . . . hoping that he might catch your eye and that you'll play him for a couple minutes this game. OR terrified that you *will* . . . because he know's that he's not good enough and you've done nothing to build him up and so then he drops a ball or strikes out and all of those people who come to watch these damn things—to whom it's SO important that their neighborhood team does well—they laugh at my kid. He is mocked and laughed at and, and . . . NO. I do not want that happening to him. Not now. At least not this year. *No.*

THE COACH *waves at someone nearby. Laughs at something said to him.* THE DAD *waits. Finally* THE COACH *turns to him again.*

COACH . . . it will, though.

DAD Hmmmmmm?

COACH If I play your boy . . . he's gonna make a bunch of mistakes . . . that's gonna happen to him. It's gonna happen a *lot*. I mean, come on. You know it is.

DAD Yes, but you'll keep him in. You'll keep him out there and that's the difference. He'll play and he'll get better and he'll have a chance. For at least *one* season . . . he'll have the opportunity to play. As a *member* of this team . . . as one of the guys. (*Beat.*) That's what I'm paying you for . . .

COACH I guess. (*Beat.*) Don't be surprised if I make him *bunt* a lot. Use him for squeeze plays . . . that sorta thing.

DAD I won't be.

COACH Alright then.

DAD And he'll look up to you . . . you will be a role model to him forever . . . for the rest of his life. It happens. You *know* that.

COACH Yeah. It does. I know.

DAD So let it then . . . just let that happen. I don't care what it costs.

COACH Ok. If that's what you want and you don't care what people say . . . then alright. (*He shrugs.*) See how it goes, I guess . . .

THE DAD *nods his head. Smiles at someone far off. Waves.*

DAD He loves the new uniforms . . .

COACH Yeah, they're pretty cool. With all the red stripes there. On the sleeves.

DAD Yes. I like 'em, too.

COACH Great. (*Beat.*) My wife designed 'em.

DAD Nice.

THE DAD *keeps looking over to where someone is across the park.*
THE COACH *watches him.*

COACH And . . . so . . . ?

DAD I'll take care of it. We don't need to discuss that right now. Do we?

COACH . . . well . . .

DAD Not today. On the first practice.

COACH I guess not. No. But just so . . . we're . . .

DAD We are.

They nod without looking at each other. THE DAD *waves to someone in the distance again. Smiles more broadly.*

COACH You ever just throw a ball around with him sometimes . . . in the yard? (*Beat.*) It does make a difference.

DAD I try to do that. I'm usually home late from work but I'll try to do it more . . .

COACH Alright. Good. Anything you can do to help me out here . . .

DAD Of course.

COACH People're gonna think I'm outta my mind! Just so you know.

DAD Maybe.

COACH Not "maybe." For *sure*.

DAD I don't care. I really don't. (*Beat.*) And you promise that you'll keep him playing, no matter *how* he does? Whatever happens?

COACH I guess.

DAD No. Tell me for sure. That you will do that, no matter what.

COACH Yeah . . . sure . . . I will. (*Beat.*) *Yes*.

DAD Fine.

COACH And you'll . . . ?

DAD Yes. (*Beat.*) A check's alright? Or . . . ?

COACH I'd prefer cash. If you can.

DAD I'll make it cash.

COACH Good.

DAD Every week?

COACH That'd be good.

DAD Fine.

COACH Or up front . . . if that's at all . . . ?

DAD I'd rather do it once a week.

COACH Alright.

DAD Just to keep things . . . you know.

COACH Yeah.

DAD If you don't mind.

COACH Ok.

DAD Thank you . . . I mean that. I do.

COACH . . .

DAD Anyway, just . . . (*Beat.*) Thanks.

The two men keep looking into the distance. THE DAD *turns and holds his hand out.* THE COACH *doesn't take it.*

COACH I should probably get over there. Get the guys warming up—
hand out these forms for all the physicals and stuff. Their fees.

DAD Sure.

COACH Okay.

DAD That's . . .

COACH Alright then.

THE COACH *nods but doesn't move just yet. Another long moment of silence between them.*

DAD . . . beautiful day.

COACH Uh-huh. It sure is.

THE COACH *nods. Gives* THE DAD *one of the physical forms.* THE COACH *walks off.* THE DAD *waves to his kid again. He smiles at him and makes a gesture like he's batting the ball or catching the ball. Nods and smiles and waves.*

THE DAD *keeps watching his child in the distance. Very slowly the smile falls from his face.*

Now he is just staring.

A peppy version of "Take Me Out to the Ball Game" begins to play in the distance.

Silence. Darkness.

American Monologues

Tour de France and *Current Events* had their world premiere at Center Stage Theatre in Baltimore, MD, in June 2012. They were directed by Hal Hartley.

BOB   Bobby Cannavale
HEATHER   Gia Crovatin

tour de france

A GUY. *Talking directly to us.*

BOB I don't get what you're saying. America? "What is America" to
who? Me? I dunno . . . (*Beat.*) It's, ummmm, you know. *This.* It's
us being able to talk like this, to ask that very question, right? And
to not be thrown in prison or whatever, to have a *discussion* like
we're doing and be free to do that. That's America. (*Beat.*) Think
about it: in just however many years it took—pilgrims and the Civil
War or whatever, anyway, not that long—and if you look around
it's pretty great. Right? I mean people can be whatever they
wanna be. Seriously, even President. Anything. (*Beat.*) Give you an
example: I was doing my run in the park, I run every morning, and
I'm passing other joggers and girls on *skates* and all that stuff,
tourists, and this black guy zips by me on one of those bicycles
for racing. A racing bike. All done up in the gear, with the helmet
and *Oakleys* and the little shoes you put in the stirrups. The whole
get-up. And I see that and it just . . . you know, it puts a smile on
my face because if my dad had been there—I'm saying my own
father, a guy just *one* generation back from me—my ol' man
would've yelled, "Hey!! That nigger just stole somebody's bike!!"
I'm being completely serious here, that's *exactly* what he would've
said, and back then, he might've even been right, who knows?

But that would be the *first* thing that comes into his head. See? (*Beat.*) Yet today, in this day and age, that dude out there on his Scwhinn is just tearing it up, having a great time and smiling like he doesn't have a care in the world. He feels *free* enough to do that and he knows nobody in their right mind gives a shit about him or what he's up to. I mean, it makes me laugh because *who* is this dude? He's not gonna be in the Tour de France or anything, not any time soon—and not just because he's black, no, it's not that—he's gotta be at least 35, 36 years old and that's when most of those guys quit, so he's just doing it because he *enjoys* it, because he *can*, and that's awesome. I *love* that. I really do. And that's what they mean when they say "land of the free and home of the brave." In this country, you are "free" to go do whatever the hell you want, just so long as you're "brave" enough to go off and do it—even if everybody else thinks you're crazy or stupid or, like, you know . . . have no business doing it. (*Beat.*) To me, *that* is what it means to be an American. Yeah. (*Gestures.*) That right there. That "freedom." *That's* the key . . .

He stops for a moment. Looking at us. Silent. Waiting.

THE END.

current events

A WOMAN. *Talking directly to us.*

HEATHER . . . I don't know . . . I feel like I haven't really had my
"American experience" yet, you know what I mean? Not yet. I'm
young so that's not a big . . . but does that make sense? I go out
a lot, with friends or I mean with *guys* and stuff, and I'm working
and saving up for my own place—like most people my age—and
so I can't say with a definitive pinpoint, like, "Yes, this is what it
means to be an American to me." I'm sure when I'm married and
I have a kid or two . . . I've always wanted to live in Connecticut
or at least around there, in the Northeast somewhere, that's
been a dream . . . a home in a really nice town up in Westchester
County with maybe even a little bit of property or whatever,
so that we can have a pool or a guest house, nothing fancy
but kinda like the way that I grew up, that's all. I deserve that,
I think—at least that much. Right? Because we're supposed to
build on that, what our parents managed to do before us, we
build on that and make way for the, you know . . . I dunno!
The next generation, I guess . . . or something like that. The
next ones to come along . . . whatever they're called.

She stops for a moment, considering.

Wait. I mean, that's me! *I'm* the next one to come along, I am the
next generation—and I'm not gonna lie to you, it's been hard.
Really hard. Second I got out of school . . . well, right after my
Masters, anyway . . . and I had to get out there and land a job—
not in my field, no, not in *publishing* at all—but up every morning
and to work by nine, five days a week . . . it's not easy. Thank God
I don't have any school loans or crap like that, I don't know how
people do it when they have that sorta stuff to deal with, too, but
still, there's rent and, like, *utilities* and all that, every month, the
cable. It's crazy. Seriously crazy. I do it, though, I keep doing it
and going out and meeting people and I try to stay positive. I'll
whisper to myself each night that I'm living the dream, this *dream*
that my folks had for me and that I now share . . . a *belief* in a
world . . . a better kind of world where I can't just lose a bunch of
money from stocks the way my dad did or have to deal with wars
going on all the time—I think most of those countries over there
are actually *very* ungrateful to us after all we've done for them
and we should just, you know . . .

The WOMAN *thinks for a moment, weighing her next words.*

I'm not sure. I'm not a politician and I didn't even study this, but
I think maybe we should just start to get out of there. The Middle
East. Pull out and leave them to it. I mean, we've got our own
problems right here in America . . . I know *I* do. I've got a *lot* of
stuff I'm dealing with in my own life—I mean, I come off my parent's
health insurance in, like, *eight* months!—so, yeah . . . I've got enough
going on for, like, *ten* people without having to worry about some
war in Afghanistan or freedom in Syria or that kind of thing. Welfare.
Any of those issues! I'm just totally on overload, ok? (*Beat.*) I guess

maybe *that's* my American dream right now: I'm dreaming about the day when I can stop helping out everyone else and start living for me . . . I run downstairs and get coffee all day long, *I'm* always the designated driver, it's usually *me* who figures out all the separate checks at lunch . . . so when's it my turn? Hmmm? That's what I wanna know. When do I get to stop *caring* so much and when's it gonna start being a little bit more about *me*? (*Beat.*) I dunno, but *soon*, I hope . . . pretty-damn-soon.

THE END.

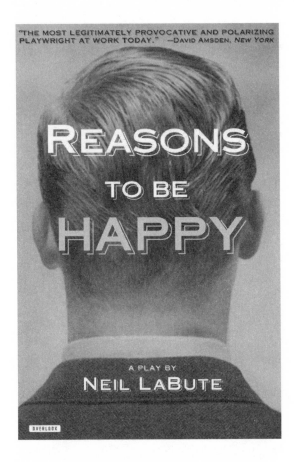

"LaBute is such a skillful writer—edgy, funny, outrageous."
—*Financial Times*

In a Forest, Dark and Deep

OVERLOOK

a play by
Neil LaBute

Betty and Bobby are sister and brother, but they have little in common. She's a college professor with a prim demeanor, and he's a carpenter with a foul mouth and violent streak. Yet on the night when Betty urgently needs help to empty her cabin in the woods—the cabin she's been renting to a male student—she calls on Bobby. In this exhilarating play of secrets and sibling rivalry, Neil LaBute unflinchingly explores the dark territory beyond, as Bobby sneeringly says, "the lies you tell yourself to get by."

"Very much a meditation on what is and is not true . . . and also a further manifestation of the longstanding authorial fascination with the close link between deep intimacy and dark violence."
— *Chicago Tribune*

$14.95 978-1-4683-0704-7

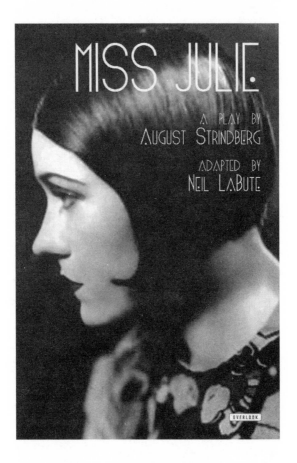

ALSO BY NEIL LABUTE AND AVAILABLE FROM THE OVERLOOK PRESS

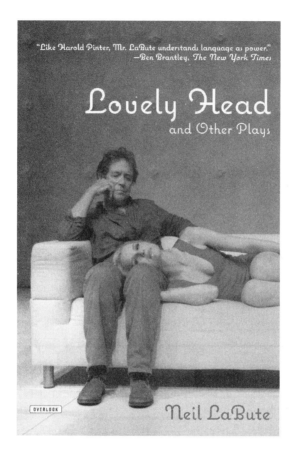

The title play, which had its American premiere at La MaMa in 2012, rivetingly explores the relationship between a nervous older man and a glib young prostitute, as their evening together drives toward a startling conclusion.

Also included is the one-act play *The Great War*, which looks at a divorcing couple and the ground they need to cross to reach their own end of hostilities; *In the Beginning*, which was written as a response to the Occupy movement and produced around the world in 2012-13 as part of *Theatre Uncut*; *The Wager*, the stage version of the film *Double or Nothing* starring Adam Brody; the two-handers *A Guy Walks Into a Bar, Over the River and Through the Woods,* and *Strange Fruit;* and two powerful new monologues, *Bad Girl* and *The Pony of Love.*

$16.95 978-1-4683-0705-4

THE OVERLOOK PRESS • NEW YORK • WWW.OVERLOOKPRESS.COM

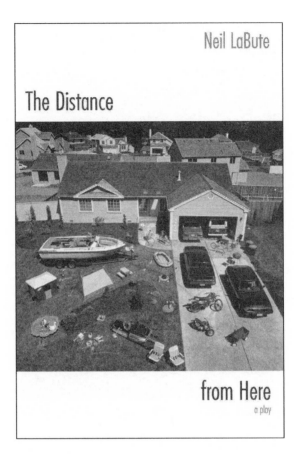

Neil LaBute burst onto the American theater scene in 1999 with the premiere of *bash* at NYC's Douglas Fairbanks Theater. These three provocative one-act plays, which examine the complexities of evil in everyday life, thrillingly exhibit LaBute's signature raw lyrical intensity. In *Medea Redux*, a woman tells of her complex and ultimately tragic relationship with her grade school English teacher; in *Iphigenia in Orem,* a Utah businessman confides in a stranger in a Las Vegas hotel room, confessing a most chilling crime; and in *A Gaggle of Saints*, a young Mormon couple separately recounts the violent events of an anniversary weekend in New York City.

"Mr. LaBute shows not only a merciless ear for contemporary speech but also a poet's sense of recurring, slyly graduated imagery . . . darkly engrossing."
—**Ben Brantley, *The New York Times***

$14.95 978-1-58567-024-6

THE OVERLOOK PRESS • NEW YORK • WWW.OVERLOOKPRESS.COM